OPEN-SEZ-ME

FOREWORD

'WHAT SHALL WE DO WITH THE CHILDREN TODAY?'

How many times have you asked yourself this question while caring for children?

After working with children for over twenty years, I found thinking up new ideas to be an endless struggle. This prompted me to research the material for Open-Sez-Me, the books that I had always wanted.

OPEN-SEZ-ME is a series of four books, set in each of the seasons. Every volume incorporates material from festivals and celebrations around the world. Each theme covered provides sufficient material for a comprehensive and varied project linking background information with things to make, stories, poems and suggested songs.

The aim is thus to provide a useful resource book for the carers of children aged two to seven. In addition older children may find it a helpful guide to use themselves in seasonal projects.

Shirley West

ACKNOWLEDGEMENTS

I wish to thank the following people.

Kate Davey, for the illustrations.

Christine Considine, for proof reading.

Liz Archibald, who read and edited the book. Her help was invaluable in completing the book.

Liz Orui, from the Japanese School in London who was a great help in providing the material for the Japanese festivals, and in encouraging her class to contribute to the book.

The Nina West Nurseries, in London, who tried out and provided some of the practical ideas.

Sarah Berman, from the Yavneh Nursery in Brighton who provided some of the back ground information on the Jewish Festivals.

All the friends who have helped and encouraged me over the last year.

CONTENTS

MARCH

MARCH

THINGS TO DO | PAGE

MARCH

COOKING

STORIES AND SONGS

MARCH

POEMS | PAGE

APRIL

FACTS

THINGS TO DO

COOKING

STORIES AND SONGS

POEMS

MAY

MARCH

**"March brings breezes sharp and chill
Shakes the dancing daffodil."**

March is named after Mars, the Roman God of War. This month is known for its strong winds.

The season of spring begins on March 21st, the date when the days and nights are of equal length. It marks the end of the sleepy winter and the starting of new life.

The word spring comes from an old Anglo-Saxon word meaning **rising.** At this time, the sun rises higher in the sky each day, the weather grows warmer and the days lengthen.

ANIMALS AWAKENING

A story to read

As the weather grows warmer, the animals that have spent the winter fast asleep begin to wake up.

Snakes and lizards creep out from their holes and lie warming themselves in the sun. Frogs and freshwater turtles swim up from the muddy floors of ponds and lakes. Newts and toads emerge from their hiding places.

Slugs and beetles creep out from their hiding places. Some are snapped up by hedgehogs that leave their winter nests of leaves and snuffle through the undergrowth. High above, bats flutter from caves and lofts to hunt for moths.

Ladybirds crawl out from under dead leaves littering woodland floors. Queen wasps start making paper nests from chewed-up wood.

Butterflies that have survived the winter flit through sunlit meadows. Insects hatch from eggs laid the year before.

Nocturnal animals sleep in the day and come out at night. And so from the sleepy winter the ground and the skies are filled with life.

A CHANGE IN THE YEAR

It is the first mild day of March:
Each minute sweeter than before,
The redbreast sings from the tall larch
That stands beside our door.

There is a blessing in the air,
Which seems a sense of joy to yield
To the bare trees, and mountain bare,
And the grass in the green field.

By William Wordsworth

NEW LIFE BEGINNING

Millions of birds fly northwards to feed and breed. Some fly huge distances and must fatten up before they make long, tiring journeys. Stored body fat gives even the smallest bird the energy to cross large tracts of sea without a meal.

After migrant birds reach breeding grounds, each male claims a special patch of land and sings to scare rival males and win a female mate. Each pair of birds then builds a nest. In this the female lays her eggs, then sits on them for weeks to keep them warm until they hatch.

After waking up from hibernation male frogs and toads lie in the water croaking to attract a mate. When a female swims near, a male seizes her around the middle and fertilizes the eggs as she releases them. Once paired, a female frog or toad lays many hundred of tiny eggs surrounded by clear jelly. After a few days, frog and toad eggs hatch into tiny legless tadpoles. (See page 59)

SPRING FLOWERS

As spring sunshine warms the soil and spring rains moisten it, plants start to grow. Some flowers grow from tiny seeds, taking food and water from the soil, and energy to grow from the sunlight. Other flowers, like bluebells, crocuses and daffodils grow from bulbs, which contain food stored from the year before. Gardens that have looked quite dead and bare all winter come alive with flowers. And farmers will sow seeds of crops, like wheat, that ripen later in the year.

Suggested songs: **Gardens, Ladybird**, from **Someone's Singing Lord**, and **One potato, two potato**, from **Appuskidu**, all published by A. & C. Black,

SPRING THROUGHOUT THE WORLD

All over the world, people celebrate spring festivals.

In China, the spring festival is called **Ch'ing Ming**, meaning **Pure Brightness.** It is one of the oldest Chinese festivals. People sweep their ancestors' graves, eat special meals, and rekindle hearth fires.

In England, Morris dancing is popular in some areas in springtime. It is thought to come from the sacrificial spring dances that took place all over Europe over two thousand years ago.

The Britannia Coconut Dancers of Bacup, Lancashire, England, blacken their faces, wear white barrel skirts and black breeches. They are led by the whiffler, who whips away winter and ill fortune.

Most Morris dancers wear bells, but the Britannia Coconut Dancers wear little discs of wood which they attach to their hands, knees and belt and clap together.

The Bampton Morris Men perform in their town in Oxten on spring bank holiday. They are accompanied by the traditional fiddler, the fool with the bladder on a stick, and a swordbearer. The swordbearer has a large plum cake on his sword, pieces of which he distributes for luck.

In India, the festival of **Holi** is held by Hindus in late March early February at the time of the Indian spring harvest. Fire and bright colours are the distinctive features of this celebration. (See page 29)

Sikhs celebrate **Hola-Mohalla**, this is a time for sport and physical games at a fair which lasts three days.

In Iran, No Ruz celebrates the beginning of the New Year and the first day of spring.
(See page 25)

In North India and Pakistan, the spring festival is called **Baswant**, which in Sanskrit means yellow, the sacred colour of India and a symbol of spring. Picnics and kite flying competitions form part of this festive day. Couples in love make this a special day of the year like Valentine's Day in Britain.
(See page 36)

The Japanese spring festival is called **Setsubun** or **Change of Season** and is celebrated on February 3rd. Ceremonies in homes and temples take place. Roast beans are scattered around in the belief that evil spirits will be driven away, allowing the new season to start well.

In Russia, their farewell festival to the winter is called **Maslenitsa**. These celebrations last for a whole week and in strict order:

On Monday - meeting
Tuesday - flirting, games and playing
Wednesday - treats and pancakes
Thursday - onslaught, plays
Friday - party for mothers-in-law
Saturday - sitting and speaking
Sunday - the farewell day

During Maslenitsa, carnivals, games, walking competitions and the burning of straw scarecrows take place.

Suggested songs: **Spring is coming, New Life in Spring,** from **Festivals (all the year)** by Jean Gilbert, published by Oxford University Press.

HOT CROSS BUNS

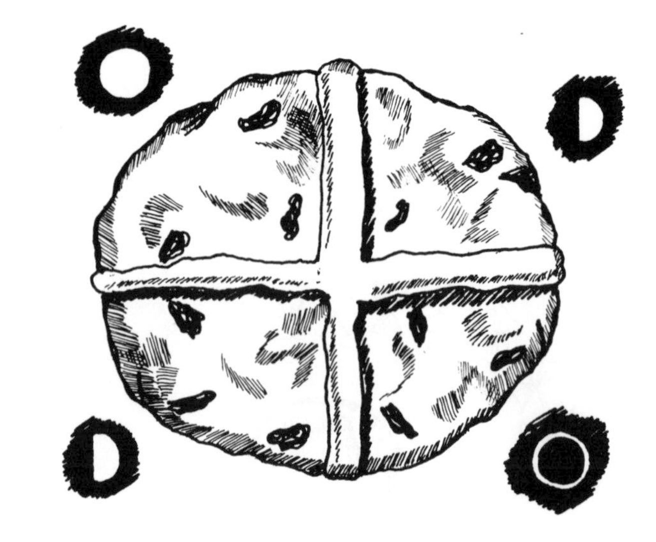

Hot cross buns are small wheaten cakes with a cross on the top which marks the bun into four sections. The buns date back to Roman times when they were eaten as part of spring celebrations, the four sections representing the four phases of the moon. As part of the Easter festival, the cross on the bun is now taken to symbolise the Cross of Christ.

In days gone by hot cross buns were believed to have holy powers. If you hung one from the ceiling, the house and all within would be protected. If someone was ill, you had to grate a small amount into warm milk or water. This was thought to cure most ailments. It was believed that if the bun went mouldy, then disaster would strike the house during the coming year.

HOT CROSS BUNS

Hot cross buns, hot cross buns!
One-a-penny, two-a-penny,
Hot cross buns.
If you have no daughters,
Give them to your sons.
One-a-penny, two-a-penny,
Hot cross buns!.
But if you have none of these little elves,
Then you may eat them yourselves.

THE HARE AND THE TORTOISE

A rabbit raced a turtle
You know the turtle won
And Mister Bunny came in late
A little hot cross bun!

THINGS TO DO

BUN GAME

Why not hang buns around the room and the children can have fun trying to eat them with their hands behind their backs.

'Hang a bun by a string
And good luck it will bring!'

The good luck bun was supposed to hang from the ceiling from one Good Friday to the next one.

A hot cross bun called the Widow's Son, has been hung in a public house in the London Docklands every Good Friday since the early 19th century.

The Widow's Bun commemorates a poor widow who originally lived on the site now occupied by the pub. Every Good Friday she baked a hot cross bun for her sailor son, who alas never came home. Part of the agreement when the pub was built was that a sailor should hang a bun each year in memory of the widow's devotion.

COOKING

HOT CROSS BUNS

YOU WILL NEED

350 g (12 oz) plain flour
110 g (4 oz) currants
25 g (1 oz) margarine
50 g (2 oz) sugar
125 ml (1/4 pt) milk sweetened with 1 sugar
7g (1/4 oz) dried yeast
5 ml teaspoon salt
5 ml teaspoon mixed spice
5 ml teaspoon ground cinnamon
1/2 5 ml teaspoon ground nutmeg
1 egg, beaten

Sugar glaze

5 ml teaspoon sugar boiled
with 1 tablespoon water.

Oven temperature: 220 'C/425 'F/Gas 7

METHOD

1. Activate yeast with the sweetened milk.

2. Sieve flour and salt, rub in fat, add sugar, spices and fruit.

3. Add yeast and egg to the dry ingredients. Use a little more milk if necessary to make a soft dough, cover and leave in a warm place to double in size.

4. Knead until smooth, divide into 12 pieces, shape into rounds, and place on greased baking trays. Mark each bun with a cross cut. Leave to prove for 15-20 minutes.

5. Re-cut crosses and bake for about 15 minutes. When cooked, brush with sugar glaze.

PANCAKE DAY

Pancakes are associated with the day before Lent, Shrove Tuesday. Traditionally this is the day for eating pancakes. The custom grew from the days before refrigeration when foods such as eggs, butter and oils had to be used up before the Lenten fast began.

PANCAKES

Mix a pancake,
Stir a pancake,
Pop it in the pan;
Fry the pancake,
Toss the pancake,
Catch it if you can.

By Christina Rossetti

PANCAKE DAY RACE IN OLNEY

This race is exclusively for women no younger than sixteen. Each competitor must wear a skirt with an apron over it and a scarf on her head. She must carry a hot frying pan in her hand, with a pancake ready for tossing.

The origin of the race is believed to come from a woman in Olney who was trying to use all her eggs before Lent began. She was interrupted by the shriving bell calling all to receive absolution, and ran to church with frying pan and batter in her hand. The bell is known locally as the Pancake Bell.

Then over twenty years ago the villagers of Olney were challenged to a race by the people of Liberal, in Kansas, USA.

The Olney women won and this led to the institution of a pancake race as an annual event on both sides of the Atlantic.

There was a time when children raced from door to door on Shrove Tuesday, cadging treats from the neighbours and chanting this rhyme:

Pancakes!
Pancakes!
Don't let the pancakes
Frizzle away.

Today the boys at Westminster School London still scramble for the pancake on Shrove Tuesday, chanting:

Pancakes!
Pancakes!
Pancake Day!
If you don't give us any
We'll all run away.

COOKING

PANCAKES

YOU WILL NEED

110 g (4 oz) plain flour
a large pinch of salt
1 egg
250 ml (1/2 pt) - half milk, half water
1 tablespoon of cooking oil
cooking oil for frying the pancakes

METHOD

1. Sift the flour and salt into a mixing bowl. Add the egg and half the liquid. Beat to a smooth batter. Stir in the rest of the liquid and the tablespoon of cooking oil and pour into a jug.

2. Heat a little oil to cover the bottom of the pan. Pour enough batter to coat the pan thinly. Fry the pancake briskly, then toss and fry the other side. Turn out on to a plate and serve with caster sugar and lemon juice.

A RECIPE FOR CREPES

The French love to eat their Crêpes with jam, butter or cheese. According to an old custom, it is believed that if you flip the Crêpes quickly in the skillet with one hand and you have a coin in the other hand, you will have good luck and money all year long!

YOU WILL NEED

1 cup (240 ml) water
1 cup (240 ml) cold milk
4 eggs
1/2 teaspoon (2 1/2 ml) salt
2 cups (480 ml) sifted flour
4 tablespoons (60 ml) melted butter
2 to 3 tablespoons (30 to 40 ml) cooking oil
skillet of Crêpe pan
blender

METHOD

1. Place all ingredients (except the oil) in a blender, cover and blend at top speed for one minute.

2. Store in refigerator for at least 2 hours.

3. Heat 2 to 3 tablespoons of oil in a skillet or Crêpe pan before adding the batter.

4. Using 1/4 cup batter per Crêpe, fry quickly, shaking the pan back and forth to keep the Crêpe from sticking.

5. Once it has been tossed, and browned quickly on the other side, the Crêpe is ready to be filled with creamed chicken, cheese or mushrooms. For a dessert, fill the Crêpe with jam or ice cream and top with a chocolate or strawberry sauce.

In Russia during Shrovetide, which they call **Myas lanitza** (butter milk) they eat pancakes called blini, made with yeast. These are served with melted butter and sour cream.

BLINI

YOU WILL NEED

225 g flour (8 oz)
2 eggs
1/2 litre milk
salt and sugar to taste
margarine for frying

METHOD

1. Mix all the ingredients together to form a batter.

2. Heat the margarine in a small frying pan and scoop enough batter to cover the bottom of the pan and cook either side.

3. Serve with melted butter and sour cream.

THIN PANCAKES Bao Bing from China

YOU WILL NEED

350 g (12 oz) flour
1 teaspoon salt
cooking oil
beansprouts

METHOD

1. Sift the flour with the salt. Add enough hot water (about 1/2 cup) to make soft dough.

2. Divide into 24 small balls. Flatten each ball until it is 5 cm (2") in diameter.

3. Brush the top one with oil and put another over it. Roll together with a rolling pin to make a pancake 15 cm (6") diameter. Repeat until there are 12 pancakes.

4. Heat a heavy pan and bake each pancake on both sides. Keep the cooked pancake wrapped in a cloth on a warmed dish.

5. Cook the bean sprouts in water for 5 minutes.

6. When ready to be eaten, peel each pancake into two. The oil layer has allowed them to separate. Put a little dish of the bean sprouts and eggs on the pancake. Fold over one end and roll up.

ASH WEDNESDAY

February 4th - March 11th

This is the first day of Lent. Traditionally it was time for penance and fasting in memory of Christ's fast in the desert. In the Roman Catholic Church the congregation receives a cross marked on the forehead with the ashes obtained by burning the palms used on the previous Palm Sunday in memory of Christ. The small crosses made from strands of palm fronds are an old symbol of grief and mourning.

THINGS TO DO

PAPER NUNS

French children made a little paper nun to mark off the Lenten weeks.

YOU WILL NEED

card, crayons

METHOD

1. Draw and cut out an outline of a nun on the card. Give her seven feet, one for each week during Lent. All feet must be facing the same way. Her arms and hands are always folded in prayer.

2. Don't give her a mouth because this is a reminder that lent is a time of fasting. Turn one little foot under her gown as each week passes.

Before calendars people invented ways to mark off the passing weeks of Lent. Greek children made a **Kukaras**. This is made from a large potato tied with ribbon with seven feathers stuck in it, one for each week of Lent. They are hung in the doorway of the kitchen. For each week that goes by one feather is pulled out.

Suggested songs: **Shrove Tuesday, Pancake Tuesday,** from **A Musical Calendar of Festivals**, published by Ward Lock Educational.

NO-RUZ

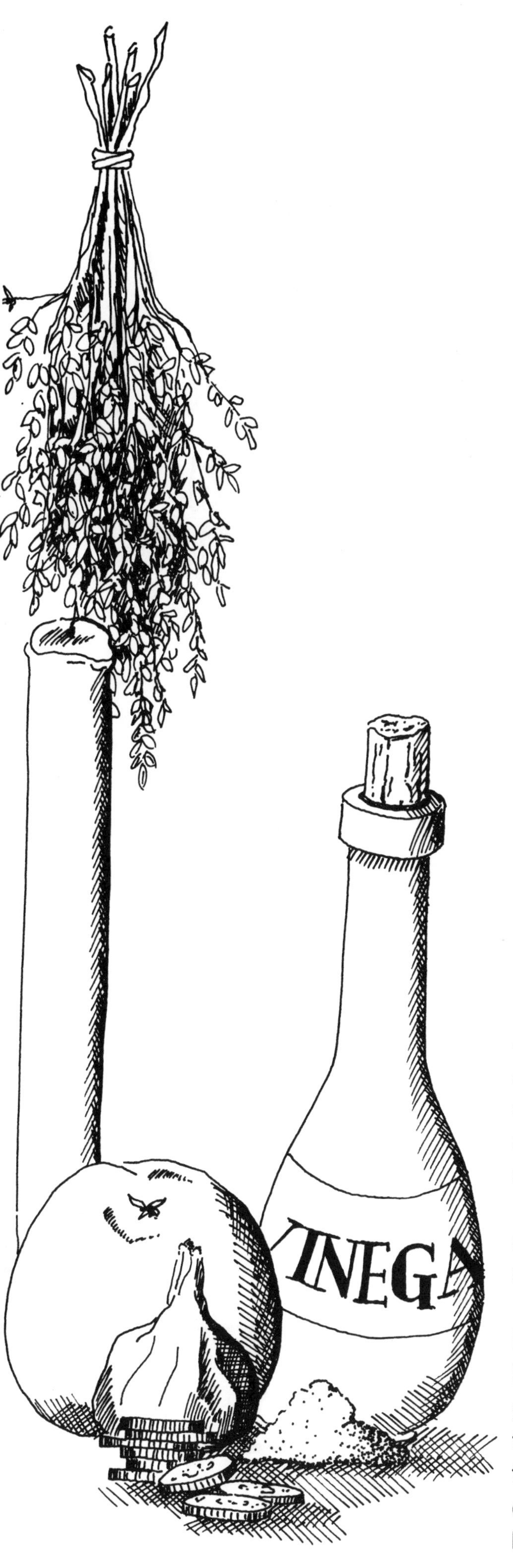

From March 21st, lasting twelve days

No-Ruz or New Year's, Day is the first day of spring in Iran (formerly Persia) which is a Muslim country. The observance is a very old one, dating back to old Persia and pre-Islamic times. The old Persian religion was Zoroastrianism, named after its founder, Zoroaster. Ahura Mazda was believed to be the supreme god.

The week before the festival begins **kahneh takani** (the house-shaking, or cleaning) takes place. A day or two before No-Ruz the whole family goes to the public bath.

When the sun crosses the equator the new year begins. Families, bare footed and dressed in their new clothing, gather together around a table. On the table are placed the bowls of growing cereal and a tray with at least seven foods beginning with the Persian letter **S** (haft sin), which are symbols of the goodness of Allah.

sabzeh - herbs
serkeh - vinegar
seeb - apple
sir - garlic (to chase away the evil spirits)
somaq - a crystalline lemon-tasting spice
(a symbol of good life),
samanoo (a sweet pudding)
sekeh - gold or silver (a symbol wealth)

For each member of the family there is a lighted candle, and if possible, a goldfish in a glass bowl. It is believed that at the moment the new year changes, the fish turns over in the water. Then the gun or canon goes off, and each person says, **'May your new year be blessed!'**

CHAHAR SHANBEH SORI

The last Wednesday before No-Ruz is known as **Chahar Shanbeh Sori**. On this day people light small bonfires. Everyone jumps over the fire singing, **'Take away my yellow colour, I'll take your reddish hue'** which means the end of winter drabness and the beginning of summer warmth. The children receive gifts, a toy, a coin, jewellery, a plant or a flower.

TRADITIONAL FOOD

The first meal of the new year will include fish and there must be rice cooked in a special way with fresh herbs (dill, chives and parsley). This traditional dinner also includes jujube fruit (a small plum-like fruit from an Eastern shrub), olives, smoked fish, a sweet pudding made of wheat, as well as bread, various grains which symbolize a bountiful harvest, eggs, yogurt, cheese and sweets.

This twelve-day feast is spent visiting friends. Wherever they go, there are many delicious tiny cakes and many kinds of sweets. Everyone, even the children, drinks a cup of very sweet tea. Each child goes home with their pocket full of ajeel, roasted dried peas, dried mulberries, raisins, pistachio nuts, roasted squash and water-melon seeds.

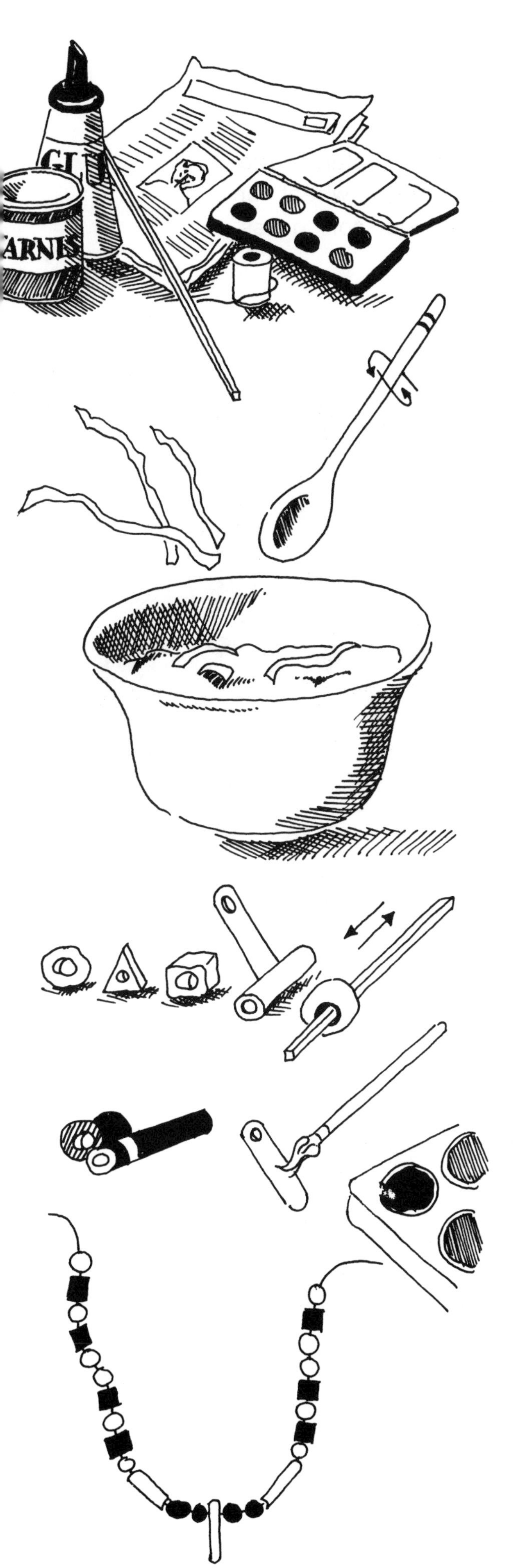

THINGS TO DO

MAKE A NECKLACE from papier mache

YOU WILL NEED

newspaper, glue, paint, thin stick, varnish, thread

For the paste use any of the following:

1. Three cups of water mixed with one cup of flour.

2. One cup of wallpaper paste mixed with three cups of water.

3. Mix two cups of white glue to one cup of water.

METHOD

1. Add strips of torn newspaper to the paste until the mixture is manageable. Squeeze away any excess water.

2. Make beads of all kinds of shapes and sizes from the papier mache pulp. Use a thin stick to poke holes through the beads while they are still wet. When the papier mache is dry, paint the beads and varnish them. String the beads to make the necklace.

OTHER IDEAS

You can also make necklaces by painting and then threading pasta tubes. Or by drying out water-melon pips by cooking in a slow oven for an hour. Paint and then thread them. The pips can also be used to make a collage.

PLANTING THE SABZEH The. Symbol of Spring

Two weeks before the No-Ruz celebration, each family plants the Sabezh: wheat, lentil or barley seeds. If you don't have wheat or barley, try planting some lentil, watercress, sunflower or grass seeds.

YOU WILL NEED

watercress seed, plate, sponge or cotton wool

METHOD

1. Place a damp sponge or cotton wool on a plate and sprinkle with watercress seeds. Water a little each day and soon you will have sprouts.

2. On the last day of the celebrations you must throw out the bowls of green into some running water, a sign that all illness, bad luck, ill feeling, and family quarrels are cast away.

COOKING

NAN BREAD

YOU WILL NEED

200 g (7 oz) plain white flour
1 teaspoon baking powder
1 teaspoon plain yoghurt
1/2 teaspoon yeast
1/2 teaspoon salt
25 g (1 oz) melted butter
55 ml (2 fl oz) water

Oven temperature: 190 'C/375 'F/Gas 5

METHOD

1. Sift the flour, salt and baking powder into a bowl. Add the yoghurt and butter. Mix to a soft dough. Gradually add the milk.

2. Divide into five balls, cover and leave for four hours. Knead each ball on a floured surface and roll out. Brush the circles with the melted butter and place on a tray. Cook in the oven on both sides for four minutes until brown specks appear. They can also be shallow fried.

HOLI

At the full moon in March/April

Holi is a famous and very popular Hindu spring festival in Northern India. It celebrates the arrival of spring flowers and when the main crops are almost ready for the spring harvest. The festival lasts anything from three to five days and is known as the festival of colour.

Holi usually begins with the lighting of bonfires which have been built by everyone. People light their household fires, and then the community fire is kindled by a brahmin priest. The ripening of the first wheat and barley crop is celebrated by being offered to the fire, and the roasted barley is eaten. The ashes of the fires are marked on the forehead to bring good luck in the year ahead.

After the bonfires comes the throwing of colour. People throw coloured water and red powders over friends or anyone who passes by. It is a happy celebration, everybody dances and has great fun. Processions of floats carrying statues of the gods line the streets.

Holi is named after the goddess Holika. During the festival, people burn the image of Holika as a symbol that good has defeated evil. This is often followed by the burning of rubbish, to show that past wrongdoing is forgiven.

Suggested songs, **Holi** from **Festivals (all the year)**, by Jean Gilbert, published by Oxford University Press.

THE STORY OF HOLI

A story to read

There was once a very cruel king called Hirnakashyah who had a son called Prahlad. Prahlad was very good and always prayed to the god Vishnu, which made his father very angry. The king tried very hard to make his son give up his belief in Vishnu.

So the king ordered his sister Holika to take Prahlad in her arms and for both of them to walk into the burning fire. The plan was that Prahlad would die and Holika would be saved because she was protected by the gods of flames. What the king did not know was that the gods' charm over Holika didn't work for one hour during the day. The hour chosen for lighting the fire just happened to be that very hour. When the flames leapt up, Holika died and Prahlad was saved by Vishnu.

Phrahlad was so sorry for Holika that he promised to name a festival after her. So now we have the festival of Holi.

MIX THE COLOURS

Mix the colours, stir the colours
What can be seen?
Mix in the yellow and stir in the blue
And all you can see is green

Mix the colours, stir the colours
Tell me what you think.
Mix in the red and stir in the white
And all you can see is pink

Mix the colours, stir the colours
Oh what can you arrange.
Mix in the red and stir in the yellow
And all you can see is orange.

By Shirley West

HOLI IS HERE

Holi is here, the day has come
To throw the colours at everyone.
Holi is here, the day has come
To start this colour festival of fun.
The bonfires are made
Holika they parade
And good has defeated evil.

By Shirley West

THINGS TO DO

Holi is a celebration of colour. In tie-dyeing the children can have fun with different colours and shapes.

TIE-DYEING

<u>YOU WILL NEED</u>

white fabric, a few pebbles or stick, string, a bowl, dye, water

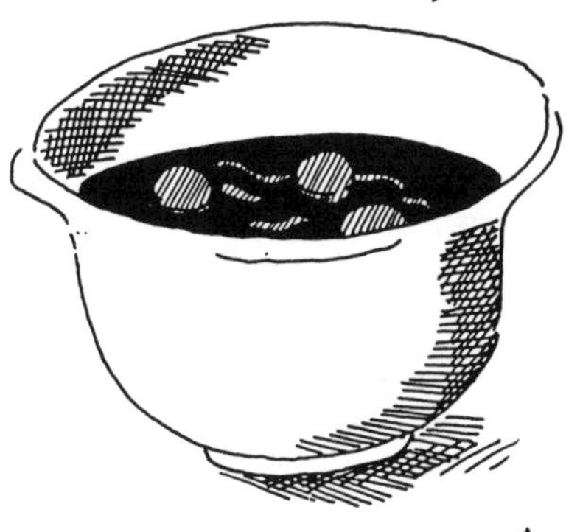

<u>METHOD</u>

1. Tie various knots with string around the fabric by using the pebbles, or twist it round a stick and tie with string.

2. Put some dye in the water. Place the fabric in the bowl for about 5 minutes. Take out, rinse and then dry.

3. In order to make another colour, tie the knots in different places and repeat steps 1 and 2. If mixing colours, begin with the lightest.

FLAME PICTURES

YOU WILL NEED

paper, large sheet of paper, red and yellow paint, shiny red and yellow paper, twigs, sponge

METHOD

1. Cut out flame shapes, and paint them red or yellow.

2. Cut the shiny paper into small pieces and glue them on to the flames. Sponge paint the large sheet of paper in bright red and yellow.

4. When this is dry create a bonfire. Glue the twigs at the bottom and the flames above.

ICING SUGAR PICTURE

For bright fiery pictures exploding with colour, try first coating paper with icing sugar paste to make sugar pictures.

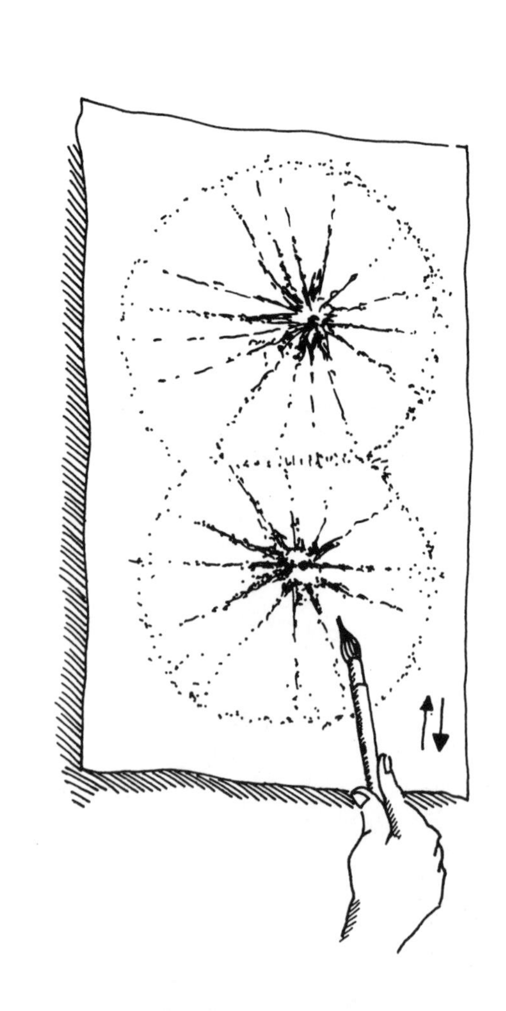

YOU WILL NEED

icing sugar, water, red, yellow and orange paint, paper

METHOD

1. Mix the icing sugar and water together to a runny paint consistency. Paint the sugar icing quite thickly all over the paper for a good effect.

2. Dip a paint brush into the paint and allow it to drip, or lightly shake it over the paper. The paint will disperse slowly into the sugar icing creating a fire effect.

Remember this activity can get quite sticky!

PEOPLE PICTURES

Using paper 'cut-outs' to start, even very young children can enjoy creating colourful pictures of people.

YOU WILL NEED

paper, powder paint, glue solution

METHOD

1. Cut out people shapes or draw round a child and cut out their shape.

2. Wet the paper with a very dilute solution of glue. Sprinkle powder paint over the paper to create a colourful picture.

EASTERN INDIA

In the rice-growing area of Eastern India, Holi is celebrated in a different way. There, on the day of the full moon, the love of the god Krishna for a girl called Radhais is re-enacted. Swings are made of flowers, because Radhais and Krishna were said to have played together on a swing. In fact, in some parts of India, the festival of Holi is primarily a joyful celebration of this love. The throwing of the coloured powder is seen as a remembrance of their playful frolics.

A RICE PICTURE

Making pictures with coloured rice is fun to do.

YOU WILL NEED

paper, rice, red, yellow and orange food colouring, water, 3 small bowls

METHOD

1. Mix the food colouring into separate bowls with water.

2. Divide the rice into the bowls and soak for at least an hour, then allow to dry. You can do this by putting the rice in a low heated oven.

3. Make a collage with the different coloured rice.

COOKING

RICE BISCUITS

YOU WILL NEED

225 g (8 oz) ground rice
225 g (8 oz) sugar
110 g (4 oz) butter
1/2 cup milk
1 teaspoon nutmeg powder
salt to taste

Oven temperature: 180 'C/350 'F/Gas 4

METHOD

1. Mix butter and ground rice together. Add the salt and sugar dissolved in a little water. Add the nutmeg and milk.

2. Knead it to a stiff dough. Take a large portion of dough and roll out to biscuit thickness.

3. Cut out the dough with a biscuit cutter, or make flower shapes, and place on a greased tray. Bake until golden brown.

PHIRNI Ground rice sweet

This is a traditional Indian sweet made from rice and milk, and decorated with fruit and nuts.

YOU WILL NEED

2 cups of milk
2 tablespoons ground rice
1/2 cup of sugar to taste
a few drops of vanilla essence
2 teaspoons almonds (blanch, slice and fry them till they are light brown)
2 teaspoons raisins

METHOD

1. Bring the milk to boil. Add rice flour and sugar, stir gentle until it thickens.

2. Stir in vanilla essence and pour into a greased baking tray. Decorate with almonds and raisins. When cold, cut into squares.

PHULKA Wheaten pancakes

Several kinds of wheaten pancakes are made in India. This is a recipe for one of them. In India a pan called a **tawa** is used instead of a frying pan.

YOU WILL NEED

2 cups of wholewheat flour
salt to taste
oil for cooking
margarine
water

METHOD

Mix salt and flour together and make a soft dough with the water. Allow to stand for half an hour. Knead well, and form into small balls. Roll out into small circles. Fry on either side until tiny blisters appear. Remove from the pan, spread with a little margarine and serve hot.

NORTH INDIA AND PAKISTAN

In North India and Pakistan their spring festival is called **Baswant**. Everyone wears yellow in some part of their clothing. The family fasts until noon and places an offering of food and white flowers before the image of the goddess of learning, **Saraswati**. It is considered to be a holy day for young children to start school.

The main meal of the day is served with yellow rice specially cooked for the occasion.

This is also the season for kite flying. Families fly kites made of coloured tissue paper and bamboo. The first hundred feet of the kite is often covered with a glue holding ground glass so that during the kite fight it can cut the string of another kite whose string it crosses. Kites that fall to the ground are captured.

THINGS TO DO

Why not create a yellow day by asking the children to wear something yellow? Using the ideas from the Holi section from page 31 you can make yellow icing and rice pictures. Cook yellow rice (with cumin or yellow food colouring) and biscuits.

YELLOW KITES

YOU WILL NEED

cane 6 mm in diameter x 90 cm (3 ft) long, thick string, strong paper, tape, yellow paint, long strips of crepe paper

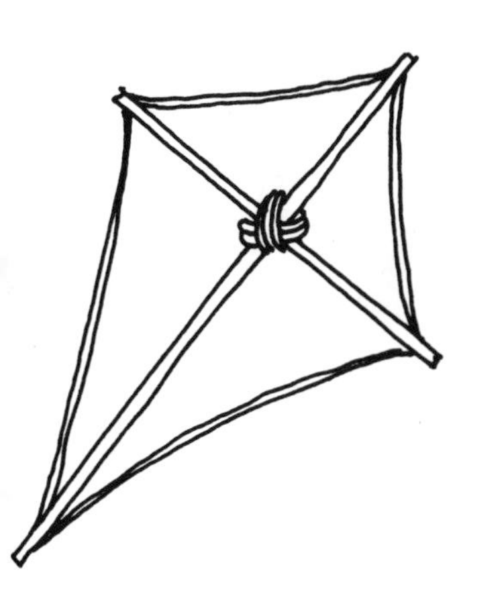

METHOD

1. Cut the cane into two pieces, one 55 cm and the other 35 cm.

2. Position the crosspiece 16cm from the top of the larger cane. Secure the 2 pieces of by winding the string around the cane. Leave a piece of string long enough to fly the kite.

3. Cut out the paper into a diamond shape, by using the crosspiece as a guide. Allow an extra 2 cm (1") all the way round. Paint and decorate the kite in yellow.

4. Place the paper on the crosspiece, fold over the excess paper and secure it with tape. Glue on the strips of crepe paper to make a tail for the kite.

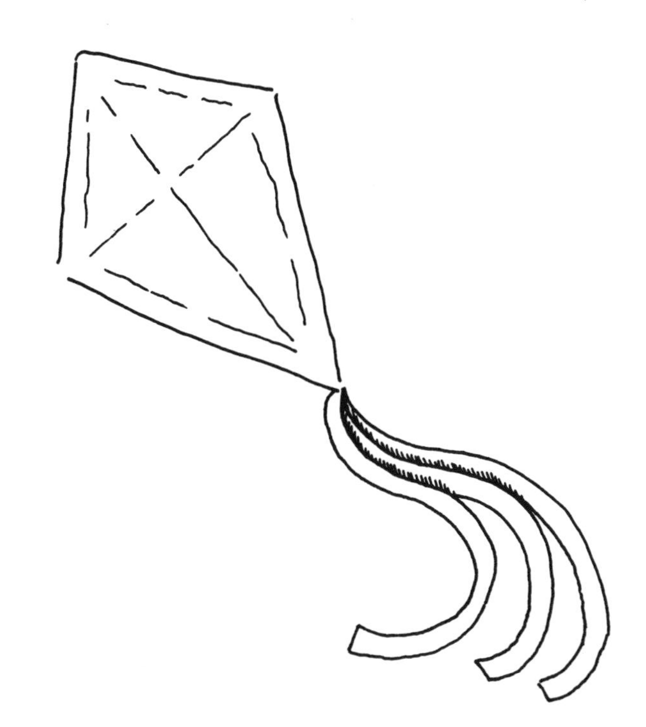

YELLOW By Shirley West

Yellow hats and yellow coats,
Yellow seas and yellow boats.
Yellow lovers having fun,
Yellow kites reaching the sun.
The world has gone all yellow today,
We are having fun in every way.

MOTHER'S DAY

Fourth Sunday in Lent

'On Mothering Sunday, above all other,
Every child should live with its mother'.

Mothering Sunday used to be the one day in Lent when feasting and games were allowed. People living in villages that didn't have a church of their own, would journey on that day to the nearest 'Mother' church. Later another tradition began. Servants or other young people who worked away from home were given the day off in order to visit their parents, and to take a cake or a bunch of flowers to their mother. But this custom soon died out.

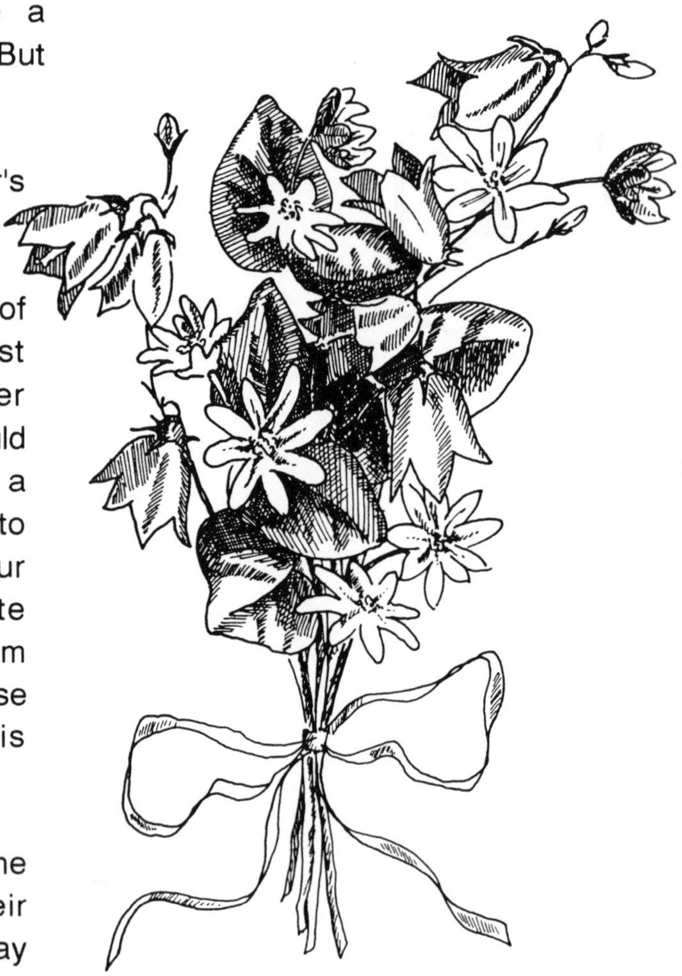

In the USA, Canada and New Zealand, Mother's Day falls on the second Sunday in May.

On May 9th 1906, a Miss Anna Jarvis of Philadelphia lost her mother. On the first anniversary she invited a friend to visit her and she suggested that one day a year should be set aside for mothers. She arranged a special church service and asked everyone to wear a white or coloured carnation in honour of their mother. Coloured carnations indicate that a person's mother is living. The custom spread and in 1913 the Senate and the House of Representatives officially dedicated this day to the memory of mothers.

During the Second World War (1939-1945) the American servicemen would often adopt their British hostesses as 'mothers' and on this day gave presents and flowers to show their appreciation of the hospitality they enjoyed. And so the custom of Mother's Day was introduced to Britain.

Suggested songs, **Mothering Sunday,** from **A Musical Calender of Festivals**, published by Ward Lock Educational.

THINGS TO DO

VIOLETS

For many centuries violets were sold in the streets of London and since medieval times violet blooms have been crystallized for cake decoration and as a sweetmeat.

CRYSTALLIZED VIOLETS

YOU WILL NEED

bunch of violets, or roses, or daffodils, 225 g (8 oz) caster sugar, 1 egg, greaseproof and kitchen paper

METHOD

1. Remove and wash the violet heads. Pat dry with kichen paper.

2. Beat the egg white until stiff. Using a clean brush, paint the mixture carefully on to the petals.

3. Place the petals in a sieve and sprinkle the caster sugar over them. Allow to dry on greaseproof paper for 2 to 3 days.

MOTHER'S DAY PICTURE

YOU WILL NEED

thick card, a clear plastic sleeve, dried flowers

METHOD

1. Glue the flowers carefully to the inside of a clear plastic sleeve.

2. Cut out a border from thick card and decorate. Glue the picture on to the border.

MOTHER'S DAY CARD with pressed flowers.

YOU WILL NEED

flowers, white card, blotting paper, felt tips, heavy books

METHOD

1. Put the flowers between 2 sheets of blotting paper so they do not touch. Allow to dry for at least 4 weeks with the heavy books placed on top.

2. Write a message in the card. Glue the flowers on the front of the card.

MAKING PERFUME

The word perfume comes from the Latin **per fumum** meaning 'through smoke', describing the burning of incense. The Romans would do this to please the gods.

YOU WILL NEED

flowers, jar, orange and lemon peel, bay leaf, foil, water

METHOD

1. Put the flower petals in a jar with some pieces of dried orange and lemon peel, and a bay leaf. Cover with water.

2. Fix some foil over the jar with a rubber band and punch small holes in the foil. Allow to stand for a few days and then drain the water.

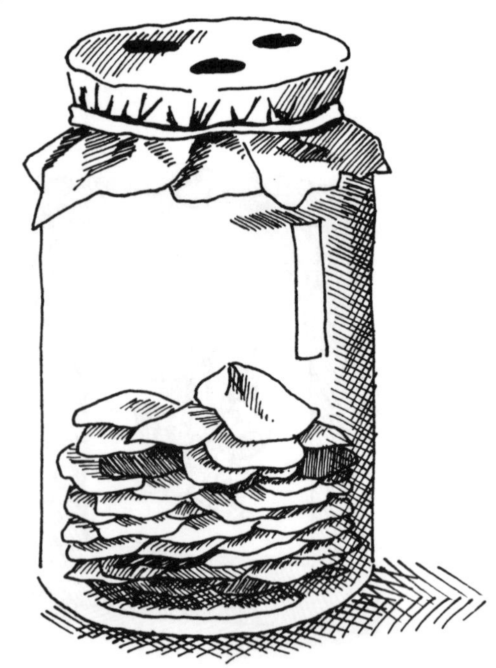

COOKING

The traditional gift of a simnel cake was made with **simeda** which is a fine wheat flour. It is rich, well-spiced and covered with almond paste.

SIMNEL CAKE

YOU WILL NEED

225 g (8 oz) plain flour
225 g (8 oz) butter
225 g (8 oz) caster sugar
225 g (8 oz) sultanas
110 g (4 oz) currants (chopped and washed)
110 g (4 oz) glace cherries
50 g (2 oz) rice flour
25 g (1 oz) candied peel (finely chopped)
large pinch of baking powder
grated rind of 2 lemons
4 eggs separated
beaten egg (to decorate)
pinch salt
sieved icing sugar
almond paste (recipe on Page 42)

Oven temperature: 150 'C/300 'F/Gas 2

METHOD

1. Sift the flour, salt, baking powder and rice flour into a bowl.

2. Mix the sultanas, currants, cherries and peel together.

3. Cream the butter with the lemon rind until soft. Add the sugar and continue creaming until mixture is light and fluffy. Beat in the egg yolk.

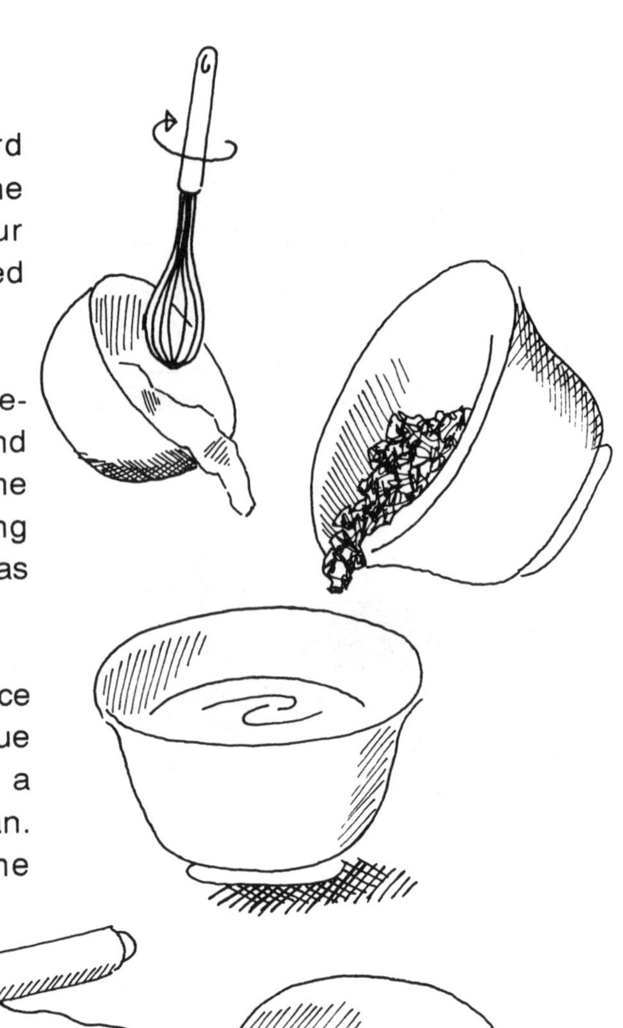

4. Whip egg white until stiff. Fold one-third of the flour into the mixture, then fold in the egg whites alternately with remaining flour and fruit. Pour half the mixture into prepared tin, spreading it a little up the sides.

5. Make the almond paste. Take just over one-third of the paste, roll it into a smooth round and place it in the tin. Cover with the remaining cake mixture. Use the remaining almond paste to cover the top of the cake as shown.

6. Bake in the oven for 2 hours, then reduce heat to 140 'C/275 'F/Gas 1 and continue cooking for about 30 minutes, or until a skewer inseted in the cake comes out clean. Allow to cool, then remove the cake from the tin and slide it on to a baking sheet.

Almond Paste

225 g (8 oz) ground almonds
275 g (10 oz) castor sugar
175 g (6 oz) sieved icing sugar
2 egg yolks, or l whole egg
juice of half a lemon
1-2 teaspoons orange flower water

1. Place almonds, caster sugar and icing sugar in a bowl and mix them together. Whisk egg yolk (or whole egg) with the lemon juice and flavouring. Add this to the mixture of ground almonds and sugar.

2. Pound the rest of the paste lightly to release a little of the oil from the almonds. Knead paste with the hands until smooth.

POEMS

ON MOTHER'S DAY MY MUM GOT MAD

On Mother's Day my mum got mad,
Because she thought we'd forgotten.
And then she got so very sad,
She thought we were quite rotten!

She told us what she thought of us,
But she didn't know what we'd planned.
We told her not to make a fuss,
As we put the flowers in her hand!

By Polly Barker (aged 10)

CAN YOU TELL ME?

If my mother went away,
Who would start my night and day?
Who would tuck me in bed so tight
And draw the curtains every night?

If my mother went away,
Who would start my night and day?
Who would kiss me on the head,
When I'm snug in my warm bed?

If my mother went away,
Who would start my night and day?
Who would get me up each time,
And hurry me off to school by nine?

By Shirley West

ORANGES AND LEMONS

Last Day in March

In medieval days barges carrying fruit from the Mediterranean landed at the wharves just below the churchyard of St Clement Dane in east London. A toll was charged by the tenants of Clement's Inn for allowing the porters to carry oranges and lemons across their property to nearby Clare Market. Now, on the last day of March, children gather at the church to attend a service and they receive presents of fruit.

A new bell was added making twelve in all, so that the tradiditional Orange and Lemons tune could be played more accurately than before. The original bells were damaged by the air raids in 1940-41.

It is said that during public executions prisoners were led along the streets to the tolling of the bells, hence, 'Here comes a chopper to chop off your head.'

ORANGES AND LEMONS

'Orange and Lemons',
said the bells of St Clements.
'You owe me five farthings',
said the bells of St Martin's.
'When will you pay me?
said the bells of Old Bailey.
'When I grow rich',
said the bells of Shoreditch.
'Pray, when will that be?
said the bells of Stepney.
'I'm sure I don't know',
said the great bells of Bow.
Here comes a candle to light you to bed,
Here comes a copper to chop off your head.
Chip-Chop-Chip-Chop,
The last man is dead.

THINGS TO DO

ORANGE AND LEMON PRINTS

YOU WILL NEED

oranges and lemons, paper, orange and yellow paint, 2 flat containers for the paint

METHOD

Cut the fruit in half. Put some paint in each of the containers. Dip the fruit into the paint and make patterned prints on the paper.

COOKING

ORANGE AND LEMON BISCUITS

YOU WILL NEED

110 g (4 oz) butter or margarine
110 g (4 oz) castor sugar
225 g (8 oz) plain flour
The rind of one orange or lemon
1 beaten egg
orange or lemon coloured icing sugar

Oven temperature: 180 'C/350 'F/Gas 4.

METHOD

1. Cream the butter and sugar together. Add egg and rind a little at a time. Beat after each addition.

2. Stir in the flour and mix to a fairly firm dough. Cut into orange and lemon shapes.

3. Place on the greased baking tray. Bake in the centre of the oven, then allow to cool.

4. Make icing sugar for the biscuits by mixing icing sugar with colouring and hot water.

ORANGE BREAD

YOU WILL NEED

225 g (8 oz) flour
110 g (4 oz) sugar
rind and juice of one orange
1x15 ml spoon of marmalade
1x15 ml spoon of cooking oil
1 egg
butter for greasing and spreading

Oven temperature: 190 'C/375 'F/Gas 5

METHOD

1. Put flour and sugar in a bowl. Add the grated orange rind with the marmalade, oil, and orange juice.

2. Beat the egg with a little milk and add to the mixture. Pour the mixture into a greased tin, and bake for 40 minutes. When cool, slice the bread and spread it with butter.

ORANGE AND LEMON SQUASH

YOU WILL NEED

900 g (2 lbs) granulated sugar
1 1/2 pint of water
grated rind of 3 large lemons
juice and grated rind of 2 large oranges
4 level teaspoons tartaric acid

METHOD

1. Dissolve the sugar and water in a pan, and boil. Simmer for 10 minutes. Place the lemon rind in a bowl with the tartaric acid and pour in the sugar syrup, mixing well.

2. Cover and leave to stand for 24 hours. Strain in the lemon and orange juice. Pour the squash into bottles and seal. Store in a cool place and dilute to taste with water.

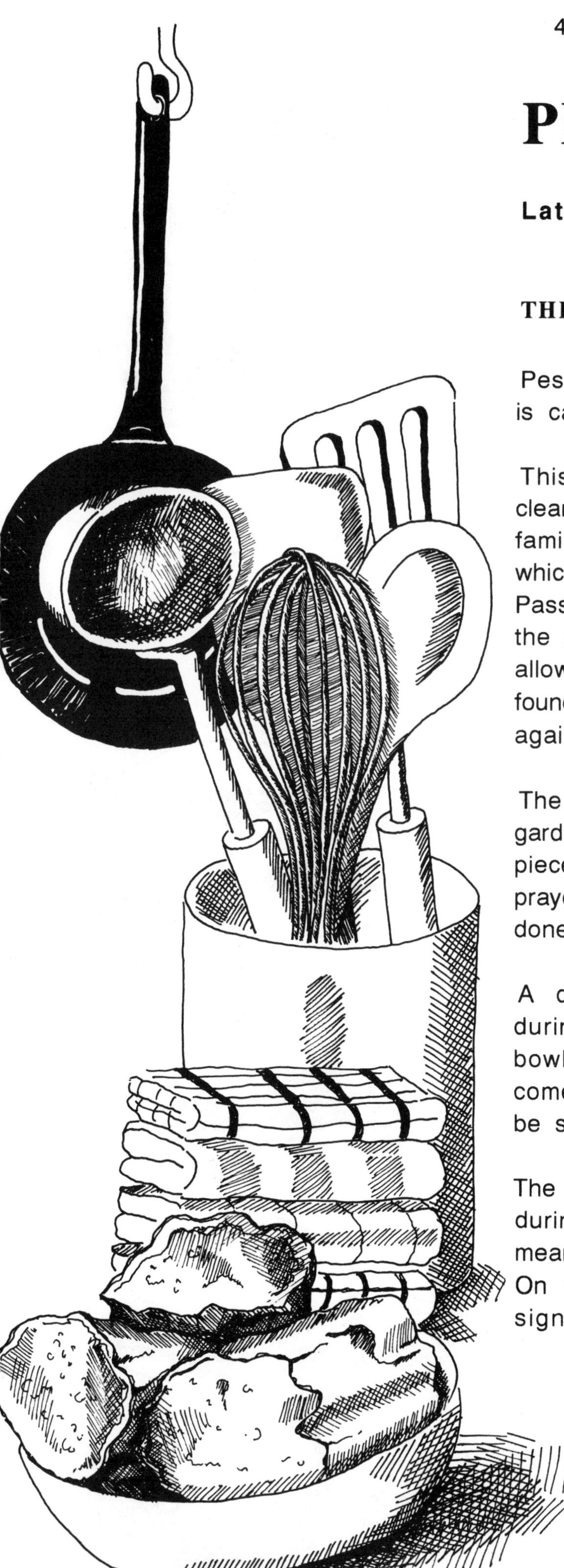

PESACH

Late March/Early April

THE PESACH FESTIVAL

Pesach is the Jewish festival of freedom. It is called Passover in English.

This eight-day festival is the time for spring-cleaning. Once this is done the mother of the family hides pieces of bread called **hametz,** which is ordinary bread. On the evening before Passover the children search the house for the pieces of hametz as ordinary bread is not allowed at Passover time. If any crumbs are found the room has to be cleaned all over again.

The next morning, everyone goes into the garden and the father places the hametz on a piece of paper and sets it alight, saying a prayer asking God to recognize that they have done their best to remove all the hametz.

A different set of kitchen utensils is used during this time, including the washing-up bowls, tea-towels, and anything else that comes in contact with food. The kitchen must be scrubbed clean.

The only food that is allowed to be eaten during this time is called **kosher** which means that it has been blessed by the rabbi. On the table are found foods with a special significance.

TRADITIONAL FOOD FOR THE SEDER TABLE

Bitter herbs, like watercress or horse-radish are a reminder of the harshness of slavery.

Karpas, which is a green plant like parsley, a symbol of springtime and hope.

Charoses, which is chopped apple prepared to semble in appearance the mortar and bricks used to build the ancient Egyptian cities.

A shankbone, symbolic of the sacrificial Pascal offering, is set beside an egg.

Roasted egg, which represents the festival sacrifice brought to the temple and is the symbol of mourning for the destroyed temple.

Salt water marks the tears shed by the slaves and the crossing of the Red Sea.

A plate of matzas recalls the hasty flight of the Israelites from Egypt.

Four cups of wine must be drunk as a reminder of the four promises made by God to redeem Israel.

A special cup of wine is poured for the Prophet Elijah, who is thought to visit each Jewish home on this night, and the door is opened for the prophet to enter. As the Seder comes to an end, everybody eats a last piece of matza and thanks God for the special gift of freedom.

THE STORY OF MOSES

A story to read

The people of Israel came to live in Egypt, where they lived and worked as free people.

Then one day a new Pharaoh came to rule and he frightened the people of Israel by ordering all their newborn sons to be killed. A woman named Yocheved did not want her son to die so she asked her daughter Miriam to set him afloat in a basket on the River Nile. The basket was later found by the Pharaoh's daughter. She took the child home and called him Moses.

When he grew up he became a shepherd. While he was looking after the sheep, Moses came across a bush which seemed to be on fire. It was burning, but it did not turn to ash. Moses heard the voice of God telling him to go to Pharaoh and tell him to free the people from slavery.

So Moses went to Pharaoh several times to ask him to free the people of Israel. Each time Pharaoh would agree but then later he would change his mind. God in his anger cursed the Egyptians with many plagues. Finally, after nine plagues, Moses told Pharaoh that if he did not let the people of Israel go, a tenth and most terrible plague would be brought on the Egyptians. Pharaoh was frightened and told Moses to leave with his people.

The people were in such a hurry to leave, they did not have enough time to let their bread rise. They took the bread with them to bake on the way.

Moses led all the people out of Egypt to the Red Sea. There Moses touched the waters with his rod. A great miracle happened. The water spread apart so that the Israelites could pass through on dry land and walk to freedom.

Ever since then, Jewish people all over the world celebrate at the time of Pesach.

THINGS TO DO

Painting and drawing activities at this time could focus on the story of the Exodus. Use red crepe paper to represent the parting of the Red Sea.

A SEDER PLATE

YOU WILL NEED

a paper plate, paper cut into 5 circles, egg shells, parsley, water cress, small pieces of brown paper rolled into balls (these represent charoses, which is the mortar and bricks), a circle cut from silver foil to represent the salt water

METHOD

1. Glue some crushed egg shell, parsley, watercress and brown balls on each of the circles. Draw a bone on the last circle.

2. Glue the silver circle in the middle of the plate. Glue the other symbols round the plate.

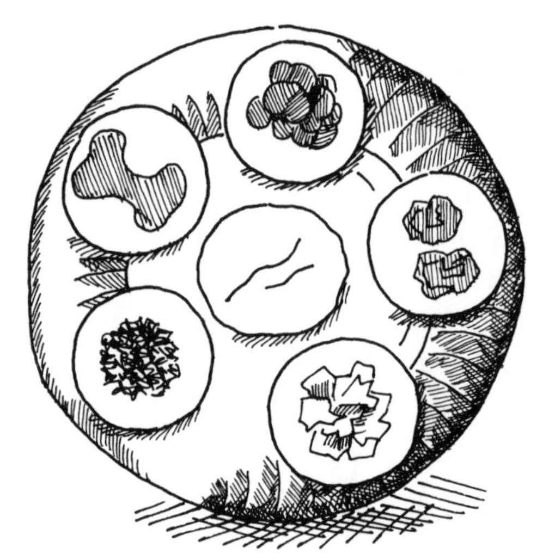

A KIPPAH

This is a special hat worn by Jewish males.

YOU WILL NEED

A4 paper, glue, scissors

METHOD

1. Cut out a circle 20 cm (8") in diameter. Draw lines dividing the circle into 8 sections and colour in.

2. Cut 10 cm (3 1/2") along each line and glue each section slightly over the one next to it all the way around. Cut out the Jewish star of David, colour it in and glue it on to the kippah.

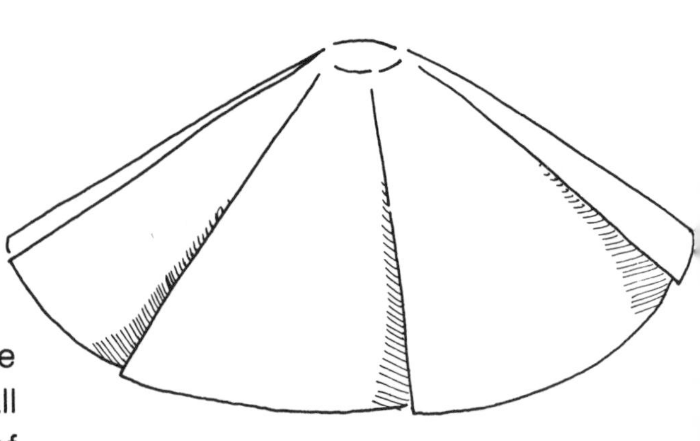

PESACH FROG GAME

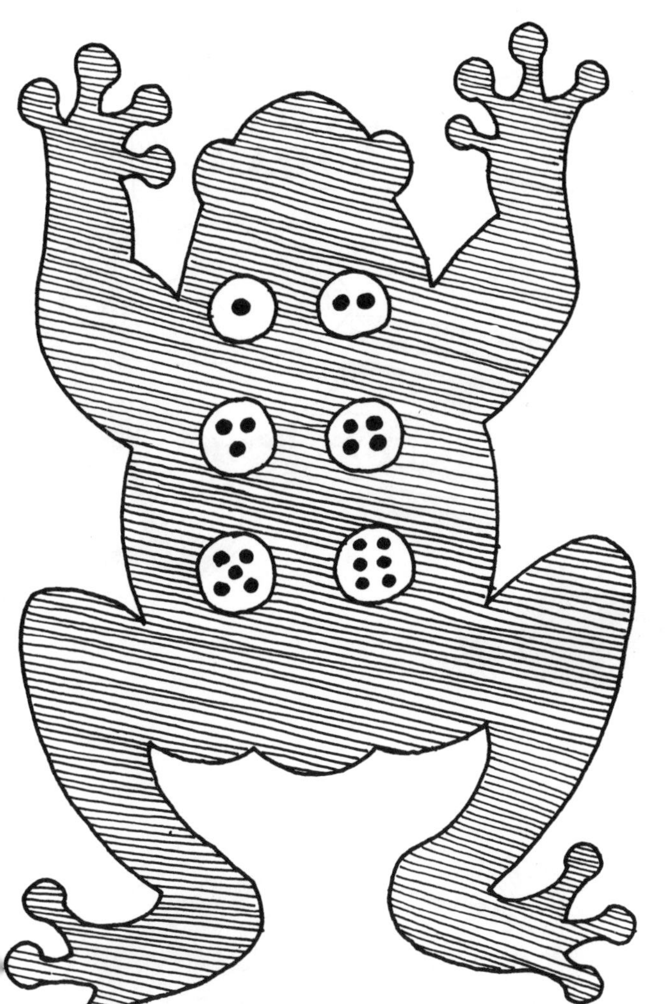

One of the plagues was frogs. At the Yavneh Nursery in Brighton the children play a frog game at Pesach time.

YOU WILL NEED

A4 card, dice, green paint

METHOD

1. Cut out 4 1 ft frog shapes and colour or paint these green.

2. Cut out 48 circles 2 cm (1") in diameter. In the first circle put 1 dot, in the second put 2 dots, and so on until you reach 6, then repeat.

3. Glue 6 circles from 1 to 6 on the frog. Divide the remaining circles amongst the 4 players making sure they have 1 of each number.

4. Each child takes a turn at throwing the dice. If they throw lets say number 5 they have to match their circle with the circle on the frog, until their frog is complete.

COOKING

During Passover, orthodox Jewish families do not eat anything that contains a raising agent. At this time recipes which use potato flour or fine matzo meal are popular.

MATZO PUDDING

YOU WILL NEED

3 matzo
110 g (4 oz) fine matzo meal
110 g (4 oz) sultanas
110 g (4 oz) sugar
50 g (2 oz) ground almonds
50 g (2 oz) currants
2 eggs
1 tablespoon margarine or fat for baking
1 teaspoon cinnamon or mixed spice
grated rind and juice of lemon

Oven temperature: 170 'C/325 'F/Gas 3

METHOD

1. Soak matzo until soft. Squeeze very dry and put in a bowl. Add the remaining ingredients (except fat), and mix well.

2. Melt fat in a baking dish and add the mixture. Bake in a moderate oven for about 1 hour.

PESACH ROLLS

YOU WILL NEED

275 g (10 oz) medium matzo meal
75 g (3 oz) margarine
1 cup boiling water
1 teaspoon of salt
1 teaspoon of sugar
4 eggs

Oven temperature: 180 'C/350 'F/Gas 4

METHOD

1. Melt the fat in the water and bring to the boil. Put in all the dry ingredients and beat until mixture forms a ball and leaves the side of the pan.

2. Beat in the eggs one at a time. Beat mixture hard for 1 minute. Place on greased trays. Bake until well risen and brown.

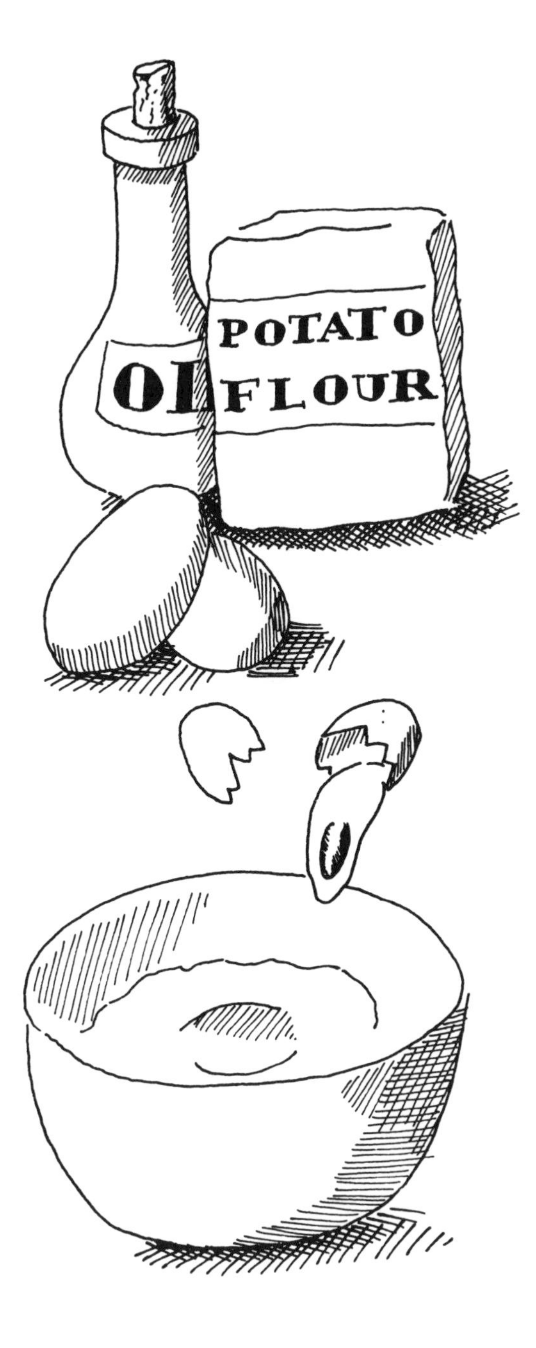

SAVOURY PANCAKES

YOU WILL NEED

225 g (8 oz) potato flour
2 eggs
cold water
a little oil

METHOD

1. Put flour into a basin, make a well and break in the eggs. Mix to a thin batter with cold water.

2. Heat a small frying pan and grease lightly. Pour in sufficient batter to cover the pan.

3. Keep the pancakes warm in a covered dish over a pan of boiling water.

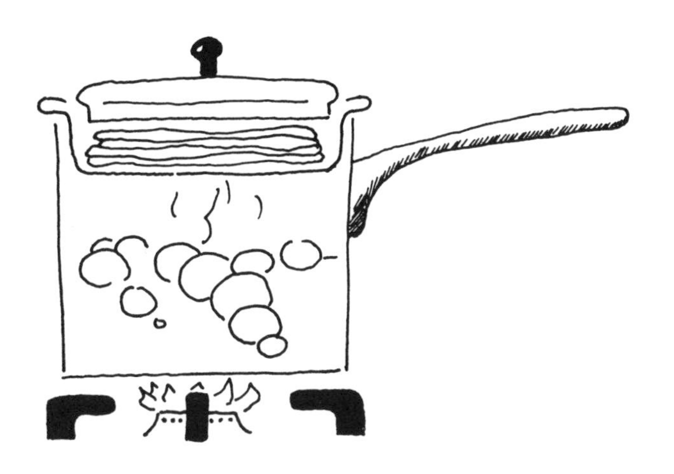

PANCAKE FILLING

YOU WILL NEED

225 g (8 oz) chopped and skinned tomatoes
175 g (6 oz) chopped mushrooms
1 clove crushed garlic
1 large chopped onion
4 medium courgettes sliced
1 medium aubergine sliced
salt and pepper, a little oil

METHOD

1. Fry all the ingredients in the oil. Cover and simmer for 1/2 hour.

2. Drain off excess juice, season and then fill your pancake. Serve hot.

At Passover time, sweet things are also eaten to symbolize the promised land of Israel.

RAISIN BARS

YOU WILL NEED

110 g (4 oz) chopped almonds
110 g (4 oz) plain flour
110 g (4 oz) raisins
110 g (4 oz) sugar
1/2 teaspoon salt
1/2 grated rind on lemon
4 eggs, 2 tablespoon water

Oven temperature: 180 'C/350 'F/Gas 4

METHOD

1. Beat yolks and sugar until light. Add water, flour, salt, and lemon rind. Stir in almonds and raisins. Fold in stiffly beaten egg whites.

2. Place in greased round tin and cut into 8 sections. Bake for 30 minutes or until brown.

THE HAGGADAH

A family ceremony known as the Seder is held on the first two nights of the festival. The story of the exodus from Egypt is retold and special foods are eaten to mark the occasion. The ceremony follows the same order in every house, this is taken from the Haggadah, the Pesach order of service.

When everyone is gathered round the table, the youngest child asks some questions starting with:

'Why is this night so different from all other nights?'

The head of the house reads the answer from the Haggadah:

'Because we were the slaves in Egypt, and now we are free.'

Then the full story of the exodus continues in word and song.

POEMS

WHEREFORE IS IT DIFFERENT?

Wherefore is this night different
From all other nights?
That on all other nights we eat
Either leavened or unleavened bread,
While on this night it must be unleavened bread.

Wherefore is this night different
From all other nights?
That on all other nights we eat
Any species of herbs,
While on this night we eat bitter herbs.

Wherefore is this night different
From all other nights?
That on all other nights we do not immerse
The herbs we eat
Even once.
While on this night we do it twice.

Wherefore is this night different
From all other nights?
That on all other nights we eat
Either sitting or leaning,
While on this night we all lean.

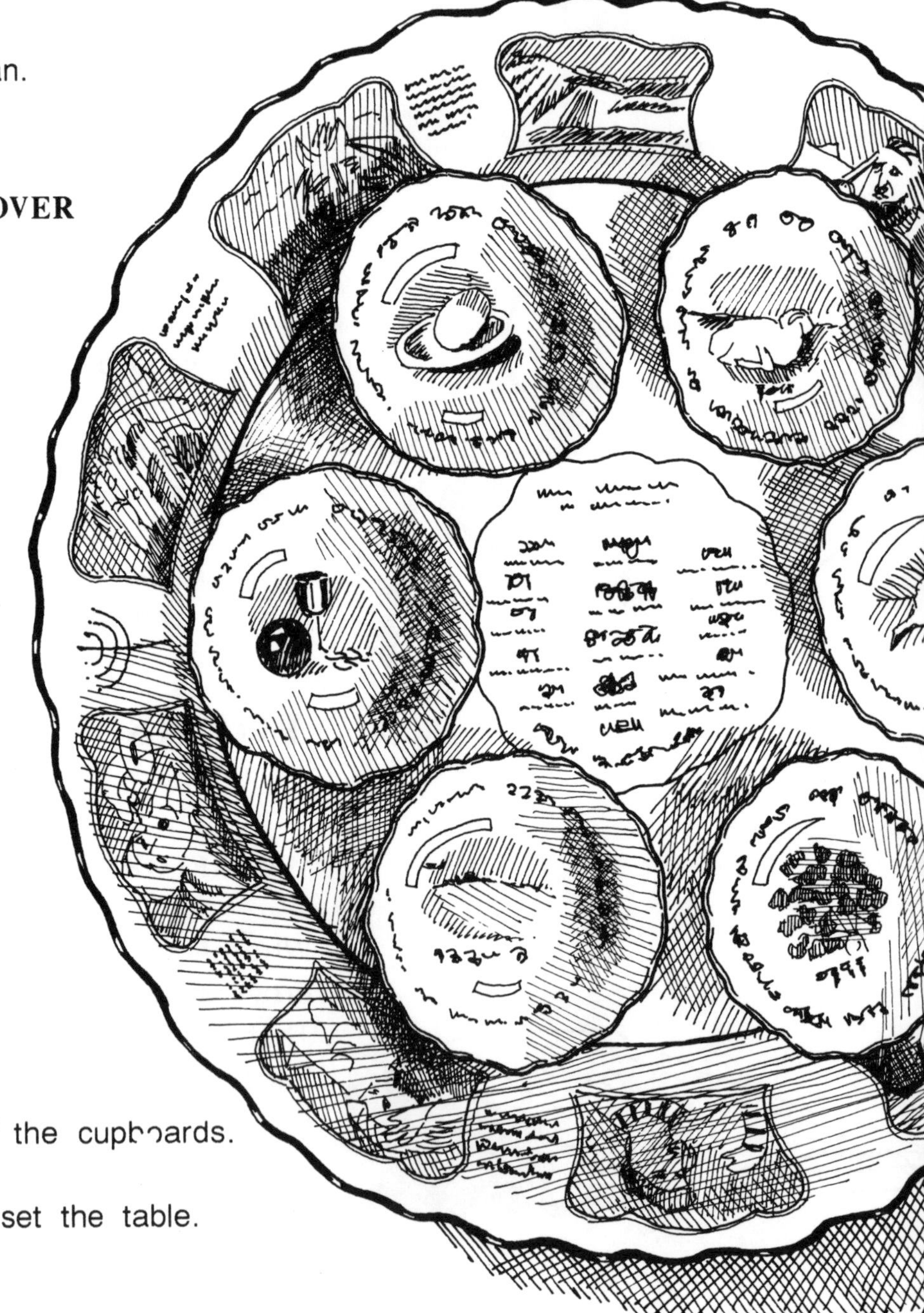

THE HAGGADAH OF PASSOVER

PESACH IS HERE TODAY

Pesach is here today
What's on a Seder plate?
Tell me I just can't wait.

Matzah's affliction
Maror is bitter.

Sweetness is Haroset
Karpas is springtime.

Yayin we drink wine
Shankbone is Zaroa.

THIS SPECIAL NIGHT

This is a special night
Everything must be right.

Clean the Hametz from all of the cupboards.
Search in every corner.
Cook special foods and then set the table.
Everything in order.

GENTLY, GENTLY

Gently, gently
A small round cradle.
On the Nile it sails.
Who is lying there?
A brave little baby
Moses never wails.

Hush crashing waves
Moses is sleeping
On the river shore.
Don't you frighten him,
Please take care of him,
We will fear no more.

BUILDING CITIES

Bang, bang, bang, hold your hammer low
Bang, bang, bang, give a heavy blow
For it's work, work, work, every day and every night,
For it's work, work, work, when it's dark and when it's light.
Dig, dig, dig, get your shovel deep
Dig, dig, dig, there's no time to sleep
For it's work, work, work, every day and every night.
For it's work, work, work, when it's dark and when it's light.

LISTEN TO KING PHARAOH

Oh listen, Oh listen
Oh listen, King Pharaoh,
Oh listen, Oh listen,
Please let my people go.
They want to go away
They work too hard all day.
King Pharaoh, King Pharaoh,
What do you day?

'No, no, no, I will not let them go
No, no, no, I will not let them go'.

ONE MORNING

One morning when Pharaoh awoke in bed
There were frogs in the bed and frogs on his head.
Frogs on his nose and frogs on his toes.
Frogs here frogs there.
Frogs just jumping everywhere.

In the end, Pharaoh let the people of Israel go.
God said to Moses
Cross over, cross over, cross over.
God said to Moses
Cross over, reach the promised land.

Moses: Hurry up, Hurry up,
Through the Red Sea water.

Israelites: O no Moses,
O no no,
We're afraid of the water

Moses: I will part, I will part,
I will part the waters.

Israelites: How do you do it?
and with what?

Moses: With my rod, with my rod

Choir: And so he did, and we march through
And so he did, and we march through
And that's the end of Pharaoh too!

Forward, everyone! To the Red Sea!

We were slaves, now we are free men and women.

Next year in Jerusalem

Suggested songs: **Dayenu, We were slaves, Wherefore is it different,** from **Festivals (all the year)**, by Jean Gilbert, published by Oxford University Press.

ALL ABOUT FROGS

Frogs will hide amongst vegetation in marshy places, and eats insects, worms, and slugs.

But in autumn our cold-blooded little friends must hibernate. The frog plunges into the water, dives down into the mud at the bottom, and falls asleep. When spring comes around again, they surface to the top and the whole cycle begins again.

A tadpole is born from each egg A few days later the tadpole will have grown gills for breathing, a tail for swimming, and horny plates for jaws, with which it nips off vegetation. In eight weeks or so the fully grown tadpole is more than an inch long. Then it begins to develop lungs, while the gills and tail gradually disappear, and four limbs will appear. At this stage the tadpole's diet changes from vegetable to animal because without animal food tadpoles will not change into frogs.

FROGSPAWN OR TADPOLES FOR AN AQUARIUM

YOU WILL NEED

aquarium, spawn or tadpoles, plants, water and mud from a pond, a jar, food, rocks

METHOD

1. Put a mixture of tap water and pond water in the aquarium, and place it near a window, but not in direct sunlight.

2. When the tadpoles can swim, feed them on breadcrumbs or shredded meat. Remove any un-eaten food. When they have legs, remove half the water. Put in some rocks that stick out of the water. Put netting over the top of the tank. Give worms, insects or slugs to the frogs.

HOW TO TELL A FROG FROM A TOAD

	FROG	TOAD
Skin	smooth and damp	drier and warty
Head	long and narrow	short and broad
Body	slim waisted	short, squat
Hind legs	usually long	shorter
The web	well developed	less developed
Movement	hops and leaps	hops, crawls and runs
Spawn	clustered	in ribbons

TOAD

Both have tongues that hang from the front end.

Whereas frogs must keep in a moist environment, toads are formed so that they can carry sufficient moisture within their skin. There are poison glands in the warts which are scattered over the toad's back. When the toad is annoyed the poison is excreted and is harmful if it gets in your eyes or mouth.

FROG

HOW TO CATCH A TOAD

The breeding season is in March or early April. Take a torch and a pair of gloves to the nearest pond during the night. When you hear the toad croaking shine the torch at it and it will not move. Wearing gloves (as the skin is poisonous), take the toad home in a wet plastic box with air holes.

Keep the toad in an old aquarium. Put netting on top to keep it in. Place in the shade, either in the garden or indoors. Handle it with wet gloves and return it to the pond in autumn so it can hibernate.

Feed the toad twice a week with live earthworms, slugs, insects and small pieces of meat. Keep a dish filled with fresh water.

Suggested songs: **Five little frogs, Frogs went a-courtin**, from **Appusskidu**, and **Frogs Festival,** from **Flying A Round**, published by A. & C. Black.

EASTER

March 22nd - April 25th

EASTER THROUGHOUT THE WORLD

Easter celebrates the resurrection of Jesus Christ after his death on the cross on Good Friday. It may fall on any day during March or April because it is kept in original relation to the Passover date, which varies with the phases of the moon. The word Easter comes from Eastre, the goddess of light and spring.

In Australia, Easter falls at the end of summer, but they still hide Easter eggs for the children. They also knock eggs in clinched fists, and have egg races in a game called pace-egging.

In Czechoslovakia, they play an old game called **pomlazka.** Boys chase the girls, and when they catch them they tap their legs lightly with willow twigs until the girls hand over a painted egg, **'pomlazka!'**, shout the boys' dancing about.

In England, though mainly in the north of the country, the ceremony of egg rolling is still to be seen at Easter time.

In Avenham Park, Preston, in Lancashire, egg rolling or pace-egging is played by children, by rolling their hard-boiled eggs down the grassy slope. The first egg to reach the bottom is the winner. Defeated rivals have their eggs taken from them and eaten.

Some say that this tradition of egg rolling, or pace-egging, symbolizes the rolling aside of the stone blocking the sepulchre from where Christ was resurrected.

But some say it is a simple game left over from ancient spring festivals, which involved more complicated egg rituals. These were performed to ensure the fields grew good crops.

The word '**pace**' isn't to do with the speed of the egg rolling down the hill. It comes from the word '**pascal**', from the Hebrew '**Pesach**', for Passover.

'Here's two or three jolly children all of one mind,
We've come a pace-egging
And hope you'll be kind.
We hope you'll be kind
With your eggs and your hare,
And we'll come no more pace-egging
Until the next year.'

In France church bells are silent from Maundy Thursday to Easter morning. The children are told that the bells have flown off to Rome to fetch them their eggs. When the bells return they'll be full of Easter eggs.

In Germany green eggs are eaten on the Thursday before Easter. They dye the eggs by boiling them in spinach. The children put out little nests of moss so that the Easter rabbit can leave her eggs in it, safe from harm.

In Greece people take candles to church at Eastertime. The priest lights the candle of his neighbours, and this light is then passed from person to person until all the candles are lit. The peal of bells can be heard through the din of fireworks. The lighted candles are carefully carried home - the flame mustn't go out. Then everyone feasts on red-dyed hard-boiled eggs, which are placed in a round loaf.

In Ireland the story is told of how the robin came flying over Calvary on the Good Friday. The robin looked down at Jesus on the cross and saw a thorn from the hawthorn crown had pierced the skin of his forehead.

So the robin swooped down, and plucked out the thorn with his beak. A drop of blood flowed out of the wound and stained the robin's breast. Since that day, the robin has had a red breast. The crossbill is said to have bent its beak trying to get one of the nails out of the cross.

In Florence, Italy, a cart laden with fireworks and flowers is paraded through the streets. A firework dove flies from the cathedral and touches the cart, so igniting the fireworks.

In Mexico on Easter Saturday, papier-mâché images of the traitor Judas appear attached to poles. They are filled with fireworks, which are lit. The explosion is the signal for rejoicing. Children also tie sticks together forming a cross. Then they weave brightly coloured wools into a diamond pattern. This is called **The Eye of God**.

In Sweden children dress up as Easter witches. They go from house to house holding a coffee pot, and people put sweets and coins in the pot. Branches of trees are brought into the house so that they will blossom on Easter Sunday. This has led to the custom of making an Easter tree. From the branches they hang blown decorated eggs. (See page 69)

In Switzerland people roll eggs down the snowy mountainsides. The parents whistle on Easter morning for the Easter hare, who then comes secretly into the house and hides eggs in small baskets for the children to find.

In the United States thousands of people arrive at the White House, where they are allowed to roll their hard-boiled eggs across the President's lawn. There is a competition to see whose egg goes the furthest. Adults are only allowed in if they are accompanied by a child. Dolly Madison, the wife of one of the presidents began this ritual in 1877.

WHO IS THE EASTER HARE?

Originally the Easter hare was the sacred companion of the Anglo-Saxon goddess Eostre, whose festival was in spring.

This is how the hare was associated with Easter. Parents told their children that the magic hare would run through the night and bring them presents. So now in many places children prepare little nests in the garden, ready for the Easter hare to put in her eggs.

In some countries, people confused the hares with rabbits, and that is why the Easter rabbit has completely taken over from the original hare.

Isn't it strange that the hare brings the eggs when it's birds who lay them?

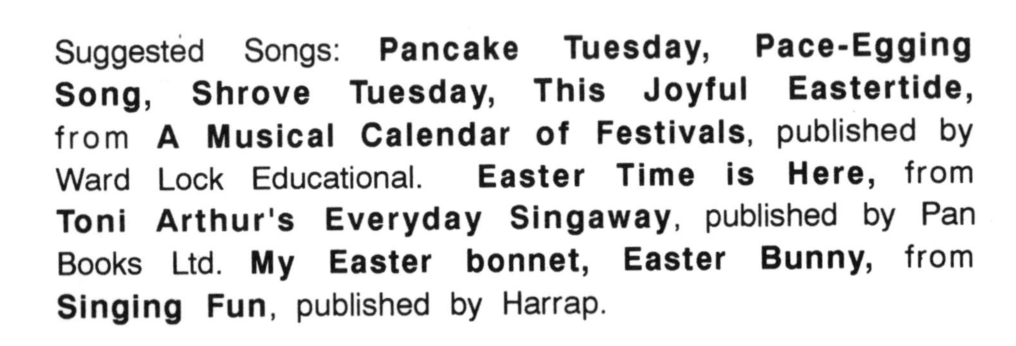

Suggested Songs: **Pancake Tuesday, Pace-Egging Song, Shrove Tuesday, This Joyful Eastertide,** from **A Musical Calendar of Festivals**, published by Ward Lock Educational. **Easter Time is Here,** from **Toni Arthur's Everyday Singaway**, published by Pan Books Ltd. **My Easter bonnet, Easter Bunny,** from **Singing Fun**, published by Harrap.

ALL ABOUT EASTER EGGS

Since the Middle Ages people have been decorating eggs for Easter gifts. The eggs were either hard boiled or the raw egg was removed by blowing through a tiny hole.

Decorating eggs, rolling eggs and knocking eggs are all popular customs practised in many parts of the world.

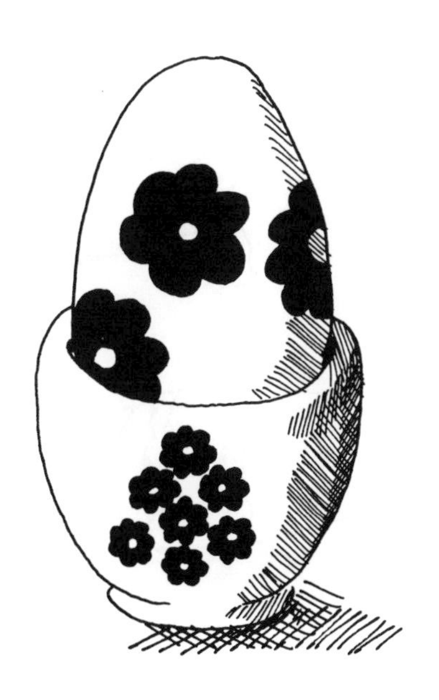

All kinds of pictures and patterns are popular: fences and fir trees, horseshoes, goats ears and cat's-paw. Flowers are very popular everywhere. Suns and crosses are found all over the world.

Did you know that the Sepick crocodile lays oblong eggs with white yolks?

In Greece the eggs are dyed in many colours. Everyone carries an egg with them, and when two people meet they knock the eggs together saying **'Christ is risen'**. No one is really sad to break an egg because the children say, **'The crack in the egg lets a blessing escape'.**

In Hungary eggs were often decorated with red flowers on a white background. The red some say represented the blood of Christ.

In Poland some women would specialize in decorating eggs with intricate designs such as Christian symbols of the fish or cross.

In Yugoslavia they marked their eggs with the letters **XV** which stood for **Christos Vakrese** or **Christ is risen**.

In France, eggs often show a daisy, the flower given to every child before Easter Mass.

THINGS TO DO

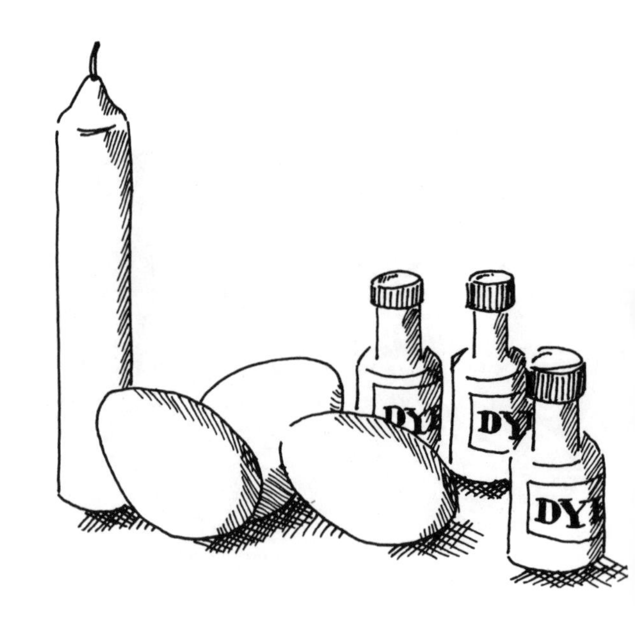

PYSANKY Egg decorating

Ukrainians are particularly well known for the beautiful folk art **pysanky,** a craft passed down from generation to generation. They use a **kistka**, a small writing instrument, a lighted candle, beeswax and several jars of brilliant dyes. A finished design may take hours and have dozens of layers wax and dyes. The eggs are raw and eventually dry out when left.

The many intricate designs of the Ukrainians are based on symbols. Wheat represents the bountiful harvest.

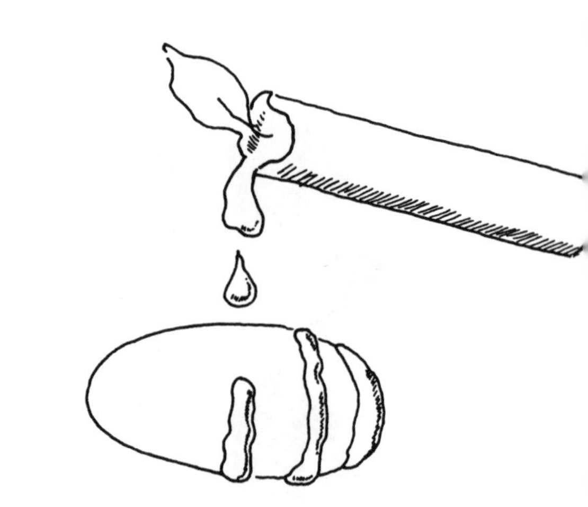

YOU WILL NEED

eggs, a candle, food dye

METHOD

1. Hold a lighted candle over the egg allowing some wax to drip on it (this becomes the light part of your design).

2. Dip the egg into some dye until it turns the shade you want.

3. Add some more wax, and dip into a second colour. Remove the wax by rubbing it off with a cloth. You might need to warm the egg in the oven if the wax has become too hard.

HAVING FUN WITH EGG WHITES

Try putting an egg white in a jar and blowing bubbles with a straw. The white foam will climb up the sides. Add a tablespoon of water and see what happens.

COLOURING EGGS WITH NATURAL DYES

Red is probably the favourite colouring for Easter eggs, some say it represents the blood of Christ, but any colour can be used.

A quick test to see if an egg is stale or not is to fill a cup or glass with salty water. If the egg sinks to the bottom It's fine, if it floats to the top it is stale, so do not use it.

YOU WILL NEED

eggs, an old pan, old rags, leaves or flowers, any of following:

Spinach, turns eggs yellowy-green.
Beetroot, turns them red.
Tea dyes them dark brown.
Onion skin, wrapped round eggs and secured with an old nylon stocking makes a golden yellow colour.
Coffee grounds, the bark of plum or young oak trees, turns them brown.
Food colouring - any colour.

METHOD

1. Tie rags round the egg, together with some leaves or flowers. This will make interesting patterns.

2. Boil in an old pan with any of the suggested ingredients above. If using food colouring, add a few drops to the water.

3. Simmer for at least 10 minutes then leave to cool in the dye.

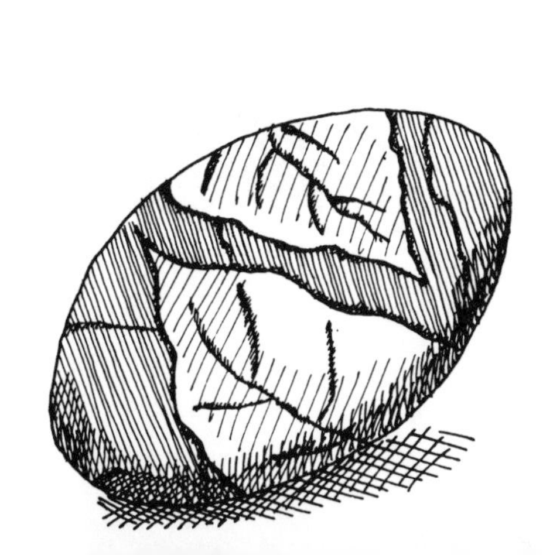

PAINTING EGGS

It is best to use raw eggs for this activity as they don't smell if kept.

YOU WILL NEED

eggs, toilet roll, food dye or poster paints, methylated spirits, wool

METHOD

1. Wash the eggs, and wipe gently with methylated spirit, to remove any grease from the surface.

2. Cut 2 cm (1") off the toilet roll, and use as a stand. Now paint the egg, either with food dye or poster paints.

3. If the children are old enough, you can encourage them to paint faces, using some wool for hair.

DECORATED EGGS

By using PVA glue you can decorate hard-boiled eggs with tiny sea shells, sequins or beads. Another idea is to make an Easter hare egg by using two small pieces of felt for ears, and some cotton for whiskers.

TEMPERA EGG PAINT

Tempera (or egg paint) was the usual medium for painting before the introduction of oil colours in the 15th century and was made up from the following:

YOU WILL NEED

4 eggs (or egg yolks), 1 teaspoon linseed oil, 1 teaspoon vinegar, jar, muslin, pigment (powder paint)

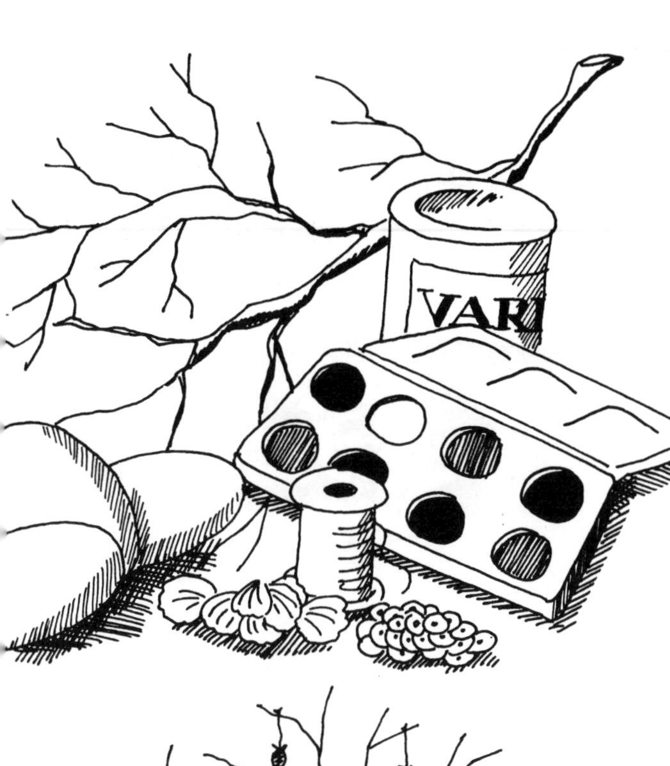

METHOD

1. Break the eggs into the jar, cap and shake.

2. Add the oil and vinegar and shake until throughly mixed. Add the pigment and shake again. Paint a picture straight away.

AN EASTER EGG TREE

YOU WILL NEED

eggs, paint, sequins, small shells or flowers, varnish (optional), thread, small branch of a tree

METHOD

1. Make a tiny hole at either end of the egg. Blow slowly until the yolk emerges, then save this for cooking. Rinse under cool water, dry and decorate. You can varnish the eggs lightly.

2. Take the branch and plant it in a flower pot. Decorate the pot with coloured paper. Thread the eggs and hang them from the branches. You can also hang little chocolate eggs from the tree.

EGGSHELL BOAT

There was once a belief that whenever a boiled egg was eaten the empty shell should be broken. This was to foil any witch who was waiting to steal the eggshell to use as a boat, so that she could head out to sea and brew a storm.

'You must break the shell to bits for fear
The witches should make it a boat, my dear;
For over the sea, away from home,
Far by night the witches roam.'

PAPIER MACHÉ EGGS

YOU WILL NEED

round balloon, wallpaper paste (without anti-fungicide, as this is harmful), water

Filling for the eggs:

straw or strands of coloured paper, small chocolate Easter eggs, sweets or biscuits, small toys, or painted eggs

METHOD

1. Blow up the balloon.

2. Mix wallpaper paste and water together as instructed. If you don't have any glue you can use 3 cups flour to 1 cup of water. Mix to a batter consistence.

3. Soak torn-up newspaper in glue or flour mixture. Depending on the age group this can be a little messy, so with the smaller children, allow them to paint the glue on to the paper then stick it on the balloon.

4. Cover the balloon with at least 6 layers of paper.

5. When the balloon is dry cut in half by zig-zagging all the way round. Paint and decorate the egg. Use the straw to line the egg, then add the filling.

1000-YEAR-OLD EGG

These eggs, when peeled have a lovely marble design and can be eaten. Use other dyes for different effects.

YOU WILL NEED

3 eggs, 2 teabags

METHOD

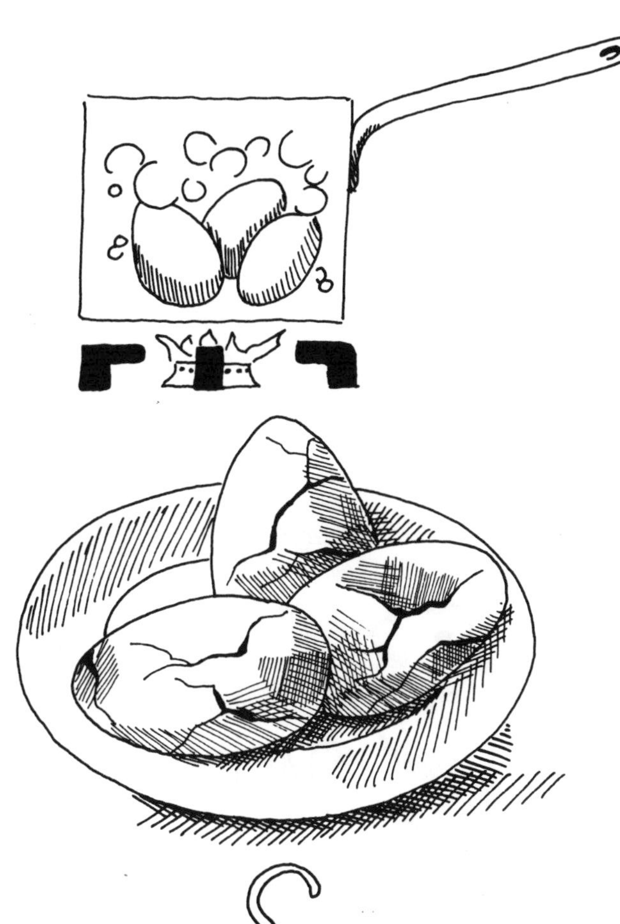

1. Place the eggs in a saucepan of cold water and boil gently for 10 minutes. Cool under a cold tap.

2. Tap the eggs gently all over on a hard surface, cracking the egg slightly all over.

3. Boil the eggs and teabags together for 10 minutes.

When you peel them, they will have a lovely marble design and you can eat them. If you want different effects use other colour dyes.

EASTER MOBILE

Cut out Easter shapes from card and paint in bright colours. Attach the shapes with string round the edge of a paper plate or to a coat hanger to make a mobile.

EASTER CARD A chick in its egg

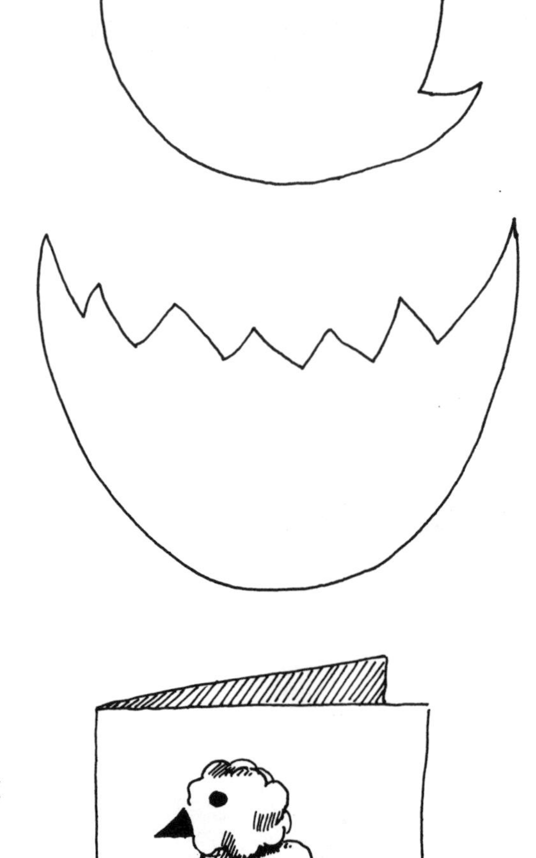

YOU WILL NEED

2 sheets of A4 paper, cotton wool, yellow food colouring, washed eggshells, black paper, glue

METHOD

1. Make yellow cotton wool by mixing a little yellow food colouring with water in an old pan. Allow the cotton wool to soak for minutes. Squeeze out the water and fluff out the cotton wool. Place on a tray and allow to dry overnight in a warm place.

2. From a sheet of paper, cut out the shapes of a chicken and a half eggshell as shown. Glue pieces of eggshell on to the egg shape. Glue yellow cotton wool onto the chick shape.

3. Cut out a beak and an eye from the black paper and stick these onto the chick.

4. Fold a fresh piece of paper in half to form a card. Glue just the outside of the shell shape to the front of the card. Insert the chick into the shell.

COOKING

CHICKEN BUNS FOR EASTER

In Norway they make chicken buns for Easter.

YOU WILL NEED

450 g (1 lb) strong bread flour
1 teaspoon salt
about 300ml (1/2 pint) lukewarm milk
small knob of butter
yeast
1 beaten egg, currants, glacé cherries

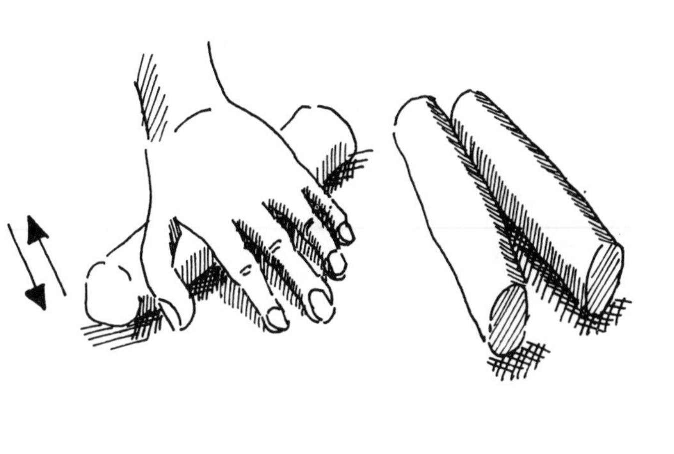

METHOD

1. Ferment the yeast. Add this slowly to the flour, salt, butter and milk in a bowl. Knead the dough vigorously.

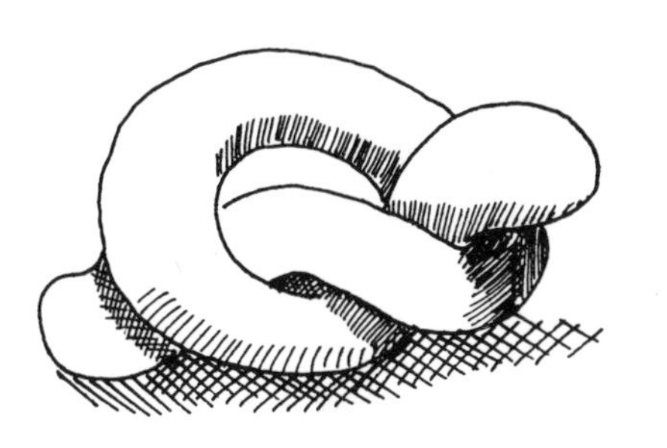

2. Divide into 12 equal pieces. Roll each piece into a fat snake about 10 cm long. Make a knot of each snake as shown.

3. Push in two currants for eyes and a piece of red glace cherry for a beak.

4. Place on a greased baking sheet and cover with a piece of greased polythene. Leave in a warm place for at least an hour until they double in size.

5. Brush gently with beaten egg and bake in a very hot oven for 5-10 minutes.

EASTER CAKES

YOU WILL NEED

225 g (8 oz) self-raising flour
110 g (4 oz) sugar
110 g (4 oz) margarine
50 g (2 oz) of currants.
a pinch of salt
half a teaspoon of allspice,
1 beaten egg

Oven temperature: 180 'C/350 'F/Gas 4

METHOD

1. Beat the margarine and sugar until creamy. Add the beaten egg and mix well. Sift in the flour, salt, and allspice.

2. Add the currants and stir till well mixed. Spoon into paper cake cases and bake for about 20 minutes.

EASTER BISCUITS

This recipe will make 20-30 little biscuits.

YOU WILL NEED

225 g (8 oz) self-raising flour
110 g (4 oz) butter or margarine
110 g (4 oz) caster sugar
50 g (2 oz) currants
25 g (1 oz) mixed peel
a pinch of salt
1 egg, separated
1-2 tablespoons milk

Oven temperature: 200 'C/400 'F/Gas 6

METHOD

1. Cream the butter and sugar. Beat in the egg yolk. Sift the flour with the salt and fold into the creamed mixture. Add the currants and mixed peel.

2. Add enough milk to make a fairly soft dough, cover and leave in a cool place to become firm.

3. Knead lightly on a floured board and roll out 1/4 inch thick.

4. Cut into rounds, using a biscuit cutter. Put on a greased baking tray in the centre of the oven.

4. After about 10 minutes, brush the biscuits with the egg white, sprinkle with sugar and continue cooking for another 10 minutes.

KOULICH

This is a traditional cake eaten during Eastertime in Russia and known as **pashka,** a tall cake, or koulich. The Russian initials KV, standing for Khristos Voskress, are printed on the frosting.

YOU WILL NEED

225 g (8 oz) self-raising flour
110 g (4 oz) sugar
110 g (4 oz) margarine
110 g (4 oz) chopped candied fruits
25 g (1 oz) chopped walnuts
50 g (2 oz) raisins
sugar icing
vanilla essence

sugar confetti, candied fruits and silver balls for decoration

Oven temperature 180`C/350'F/Gas 4

METHOD

1. Cream the margarine and sugar together. Add the beaten egg and mix well. Sift and fold in the flour. Add raisins, nuts and a dash of vanilla essence.

2. Pour batter into two round, well-greased baking tins and bake for 1 hour.

3. Let the cake cool after baking, then spread icing over the top and add decorations.

POEMS

THE CHICKENS Anon

Said the first little chicken
With a queer little squirm,
'I wish I could find
A fat little worm.'

Said the next little chicken
With an odd little shrug,
'I wish I could find
A fat little slug.'

Said the third little chicken
With a sharp little squeal,
'I wish I could find
Some nice yellow meal.'

Said the fourth little chicken
With a small sigh of grief,
'I wish I could find
A little green leaf.'

Said the fifth little chicken
With a faint little moan,
'I wish I could find
A wee gravel stone.'

'Now see here' said the mother,
From the green garden patch,
'If you want any breakfast
Just come here and scratch.'

WILL IT BE? By Shirley West

Can you think what you might find,
Searching the garden at Eastertime?
Will it be an Easter Bunny,
With a face that's oh so funny?
Will it be an egg so round,
Hidden deep under the ground?
Will it be a grizzly bear?
Oh, no, no! It's a big brown hare.

ALL ABOUT RABBITS

Rabbits were brought to the British Isles by the Normans and were domesticated by monks in the 16th century. In captivity, they live an average of six to seven years.

They come in all sorts of colours, shapes and sizes, and there are some 35 breeds in all. They have long ears, long hind legs and short fluffy tails.

The sex of a young rabbit can be determined by the shape of its genital opening. The male (or buck) has a round genital opening and the female (or doe) has a V-shaped slit. The doe rabbit has six teats.

CARING FOR A PET RABBIT

If you keep a rabbit as a pet, you will need a hutch. When buying the hutch make sure there are separate day and night compartments with a wire-mesh door on the day compartment. The roof should be pitched so it allows the rain or snow to fall away, and should be made of a tarred felt protective material. Catches should be secure and legs should lift the hutch well away from damp.

Provide a large, bark-covered log in the day compartment. The rabbit will love to gnaw on this. Even better, build a big run next to the hutch and put in a fallen tree-trunk or an old drainpipe for the rabbit to climb on.

A block of rock salt should be suspended in the hutch as rabbits have a particular need for salt in their diet.

The hutch should be cleaned twice a week and allowed to dry before fresh litter and bedding are put in. You can brush your rabbit, but the best way to ensure a silky coat is to keep the rabbit in a clean hutch.

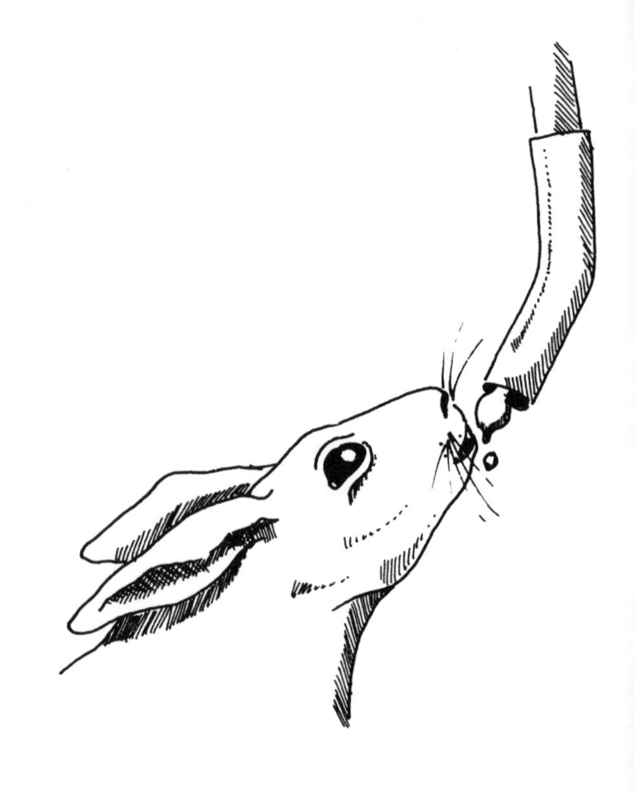

FOOD FOR THE RABBIT

Rabbits need a balanced diet of cereals, green food, and hay. A day's feed could consist of the following mix:

50 g (2 oz) oats or wheat
50 g (2 oz) cereal-based mash
175 g (6 oz) fresh vegetable matter
75 g (3 oz) hay

Hay is good for keeping a rabbit busy. It is very nutritious and must always be kept available. Lettuce contains traces of poison and should be fed only in moderation. Rabbits need to be fed twice a day, and uneaten vegetables removed daily. A rabbit also needs plenty of fresh water, so provide this in a large drip-feed bottle. Rabbits are docile by nature, and seldom bite. They should never be picked up by the ears alone, nor by the scruff of the neck. When lifting, always support the whole bodyweight.

BREEDING

In pregnancy the doe needs special care including a hutch of her own and a gradually increasing diet. Towards the end of the pregnancy put plenty of chopped hay in the hutch so that she can construct a nest, lined with her own fur.

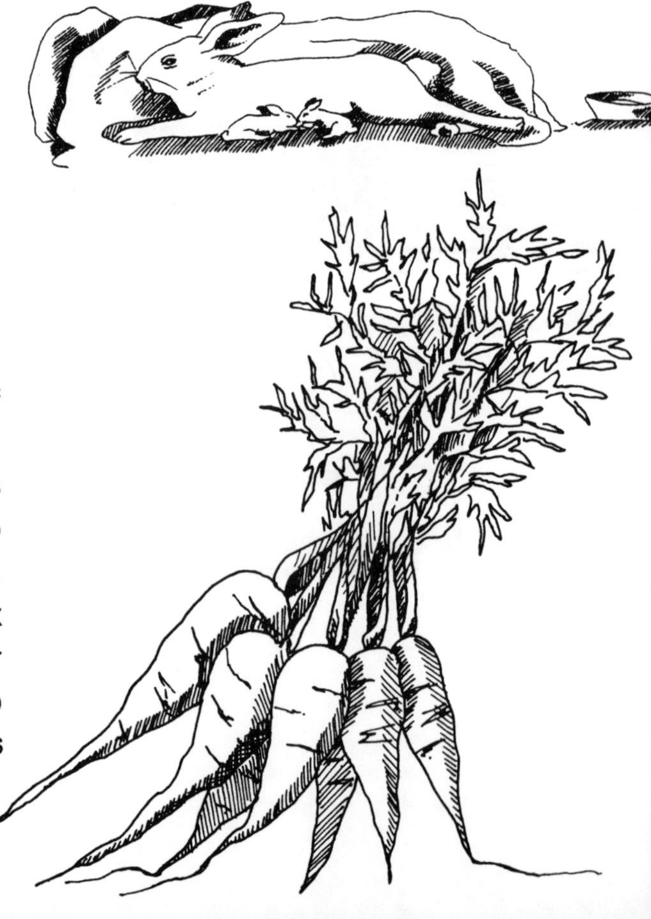

The young rabbits (kittens) are born between 28 and 34 days. They are born helpless and with no fur except a light down. By the end of the first week their fur begins to grow. By the end of the second week the eyes and ears open. During the third week the young begin to leave the nest and to take some solid food. The doe will suckle her young for about six weeks. A doe will cull some or all of her litter if she cannot produce enough milk to suckle her young or if you handle the kittens too soon after birth.

THE EASTER HARE

A story to read

Long, long ago there was a village where the people were very poor. One Easter time the mothers had no money to buy the presents of sweets they usually gave their children on Easter Sunday. They were very sad for they knew how disappointed the children would be.

'What shall we do' they asked each other, as they drew water from the well.

'We have plenty of eggs,' sighed one.

'The children are tired of eggs ' said another.

Then one of the mothers had an idea, and before dinner time all the mothers in the village knew about it, but not a single child.

Early on Easter morning, the mothers left their homes and went into the woods with little baskets on their arms. It was quite impossible to see what they had in the baskets as they were covered with coloured cloths. When the mothers returned home, the cloths were tied about their heads, and the baskets were filled with flowers.

'My mother went to pick flowers for Easter morning,' said one child, as they all walked together to church.

'So did mine!' said all the others, and laughed, for they were happy because it was Easter Sunday.

When they came out of church, the children were told to go and play in the woods before dinner. Off they ran, laughing and talking.

Suddenly someone shouted, 'Look what I've found, A RED egg!'

'I've found a BLUE one!', shouted another child

'Here's a nest full of all different colours!' said another.

They ran about searching in the bushes and filling their pockets and hats.

'What kind of eggs are they?' they asked each other. 'They're too big for wild birds' eggs.'

'They're the same size as hens' eggs!'
'Hens don't lay eggs these bright colours, silly!'

Just then a hare ran out from behind a bush

'They're hares eggs!' cried the children. 'The hare laid the eggs! Hurrah for the Easter Hare!'

A German legend, taken from **Festivals**, by Ruth Manning-Saunders, published by Bodley Head.

WHAT IS IT?

Tall ears,
His ears are long.
Twinkle nose,
His tail is small.
Tiny tail,
And he doesn't make any
Noise at all.
And - hop, he goes!

What is he?
Tall ears,
Can you guess?
Twinkle nose,
I feed him carrots.
Tiny tail,
And watercress.
And hop, he goes!

Anon

Suggested Songs: **Mr Rabbit,** from **Flying Around**. **Rabbit ain't got, Risha, rasha, rasha,** from **Appusskidu**, both published by A. & C. Black.

APRIL

'April brings the primrose sweet
Scatters daisies at our feet'

The angel of spring sprinkles the earth with soft showers, and calls up its flowers so slight and pretty.

This month of beauty and new birth, when the earth wakes from its winter sleep, when the buds appear on branches, and the woods are full of song, is called April, the opener. The Romans saw that this month opened the gates of birth and restored to life all those lovely and gentle things which had hidden in terror from the blasts of winter.

APRIL

Two little clouds one April day,
Went sailing across the sky.
They went so fast, and bumped their heads,
And both began to cry.

The big round sun came out and said,
'Oh, never mind, my dears,
I'll send all my sunbeams down,
To dry your fallen tears.'

Anon

THINGS TO DO

GROW A NAME

YOU WILL NEED

mustard and cress seeds, kitchen towel, cotton wool, two small trays, water

METHOD

1. Take the first tray place the cotton wool between two sheets of kitchen towel on a tray. Sprinkle the cress seeds to form a name, and moisten with the water.

2. Do the same on the second tray using the mustard seed, and see which one grows first.

3. The seeds take around 2 weeks to grow. Make sure the seeds are kept moist, but don't drown them.

CRESS POTATO PEOPLE

YOU WILL NEED

cress seeds, large potato, felt tips, water

METHOD

1. Slice the top off the potato and pierce the top with a fork, ready for the seeds.

2. Slice the bottom so the potato can stand. Draw a face on the potato with the felt tips. At the top of the potato plant the seeds.

BROAD BEAN

When we did this school it took almost three weeks for the shoots to appear. Matthew aged three took his home, planted it, and in no time he proudly returned to school clutching his plant with beans growing on it.

YOU WILL NEED

broad bean soaked overnight, blotting paper, labels, jar, plant pot

METHOD

1. Cut the blotting paper to the size of the jar and place inside. Pour a little water into the jar until the blotting paper is well soaked.

2. Push the bean between the jar and paper. Label the jars with each child's name. Place near a sunny window and keep moist.

A SEED EXPERIMENT

YOU WILL NEED

soil, seed tray, an old baking tray, potting compost, water

Oven temperature: 180 'C/350 'F/Gas 4

METHOD

1. Collect some soil. Mix it with water to a semi-liquid consistency and leave to soak overnight.

2. Place the potting compost in the baking tray. Sterilize a tray of compost by baking in the oven for half an hour. This will ensure that it doesn't contain any viable seeds that will germinate and spoil the experiment.

3. Then mix the soil and compost in the seed tray. After 2 to 3 weeks several seedlings will appear.

APRIL FOOL'S DAY

Tricks have been played on April 1st for a long, long time, and in many different parts of the world.

People young and old have great fun playing tricks on April Fool's Day - changing the clocks perhaps, or getting a friend to ring a number and ask to speak to Mr Fox, the number being that of the local zoo! Even the newspapers run fun stories trying to trick the public.

Some people think April Fool's Day dates back to 1582 when Pope Gregory's new-style calendar was accepted. New Year's Day moved from April 1st to January 1st but news did not travel fast in those days. Some people heard the news very late and were called **April Fool** or **April Fish**.

Some people say that the custom of making April Fool's comes from the Roman Festival Cereali, commemorating Ceres the Goddess of Agriculture and the mother of Persephone.

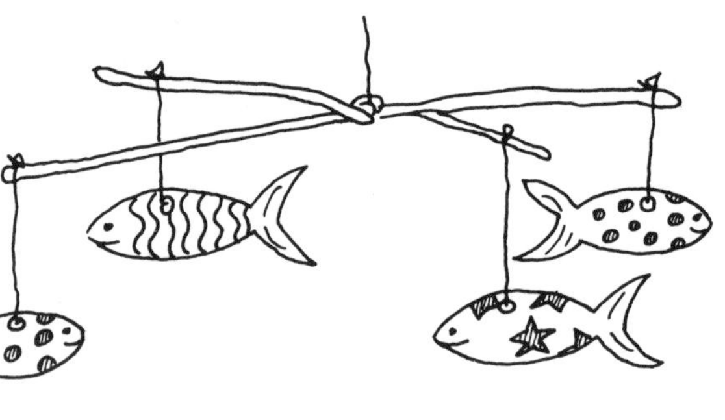

In France, April Fool's Day is called **Poisson D'Avril** (April Fish) and the children stuff paper fish down each other's shirts.

In India April Fool's Day takes place on March 31st, and is called Huli.

In Scotland, an April Fool is called a **gowk**, the Gaelic word for cuckoo. This bird fool's other birds by laying her eggs in their nests. She then leaves it up to the other bird to hatch her young. When the young cuckoo has hatched, it will toss the other birds out of the nest so that it can get the food from its foster-parents.

THE STORY OF PERSEPHONE

A story to read

One day, Persephone, the daughter of Ceres, was gathering flowers in the Elysian meadows with her playmates. Suddenly, the earth opened and Pluto, God of the Underworld appeared. He carried Persephone off to be his queen in the world below.

Persephone screamed and screamed. She was very frightened. Her mother heard her cries and ran to help her. But to her dismay she ran in the wrong direction. This was because Ceres had been fooled. Instead of following her cries, she had followed Persephone's echo.

POEMS

ALL FOOL'S DAY

The First of April, some do say
Is set apart for All Fool's Day
But why the people call it so
Nor I, nor they themselves do know
But on this day are people sent
On purpose for pure merriment.

Anon

TODAY'S THE DAY

Today's the day for having fun,
Playing tricks on everyone.
Spiders in coffee and flies in the tea,
Let's hang spaghetti from a tree.

Today's the day, April first,
Blowing up balloons and letting them burst.
Worms in sandwiches, slugs in the cake,
Let's see what mischief we can make.

By Shirley West

THINGS TO DO

A FISH MOBILE

For April Fool's Day, try making this fun and colourful fish mobile.

YOU WILL NEED

paper, a coat hanger, paint or crayons, thread

METHOD

Cut out fish shapes about 10 cm long and crayon or paint them. Tie each fish with some thread to the coat hanger.

APRIL FOOL FLOWERS

It's a fun way of seeing how flowers drink. An extension to this experiment is to use celery in place of the flowers and to see the veins of the celery suck up the coloured water.

YOU WILL NEED

a jar, water, food dye, some white flowers.

METHOD

1. Mix 10 drops of food dye with a little water in a jar. Cut the flower stems to just above the height of the jar. Leave in the water for a day or so.

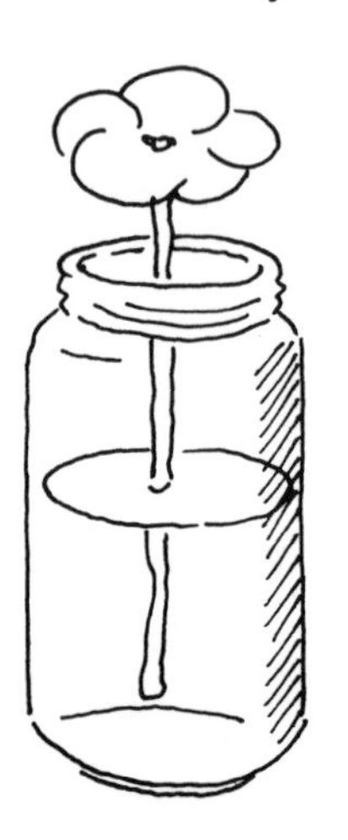

2. Split the stem of the flower half-way up. Put one half in red dye and the other half in blue.

APRIL FISH CAKE

YOU WILL NEED

175 g (6 oz) self-raising flour
110 g (4 oz) margarine
110 g (4 oz) caster sugar
2 eggs
orange coloured icing

Oven Temperature: 180 'C/350 'F/Gas 4

METHOD

1. Cream the margarine and sugar together. Beat the eggs, one at a time, and fold in the flour.

2. Put in a greased tin and bake for 30 minutes. When cool cut into a fish shape and ice.

APPLE APRIL FOOL

By making the fool red, people will be expecting a cherry or strawberry pudding, not an apple flavoured fool!

YOU WILL NEED

450 g (1 lb) apples
150 ml (1/4 pt) custard
150 ml (1/4 pt) cream
lemon juice
sugar to taste red colouring

METHOD

1. Stew the apples in very little water with the sugar, then sieve. Fold the puree into the custard. Add a few drops of lemon juice and food colouring.

2. Turn into small dessert dishes, place in the fridge. Decorate with chopped nuts.

THE WISE FOOLS OF GOTHAM

A story to read

This is the story of how the village of Gotham came to be linked with **Wise Fools**.

One day, King John was on his way to visit Gotham meadow. He was told that the people of Gotham would not welcome him.

In those days, when the king passed over a piece of land, it often became a public road. The Gotham folk liked their peaceful meadow and this was why they did not want the king to visit them. The king became angry, and he sent some of his soldiers on ahead to find out what was going on in Gotham.

When they reached the village the soldiers saw some people at the river making a terrible din. They had an eel on a string and told the soldiers that they were trying to drown it in the river. How strange!

Further on, the soldiers found some people building a hedge round a bush A cuckoo had settled on it, and they told the soldiers that they were trying to stop the cuckoo flying away. How strange!

Turning round, the soldiers then saw some people trying to rake the moon's reflection out of the village pond. How strange!

The soldiers went back to the king and told him what they had seen. The king said 'Those people of Gotham are silly fools - I shall not waste my time visiting them.

And so the people of Gotham kept their peaceful meadow. The truth is, if they were fools at all, they were very wise fools.

By Shirley West

WORLD HEALTH DAY

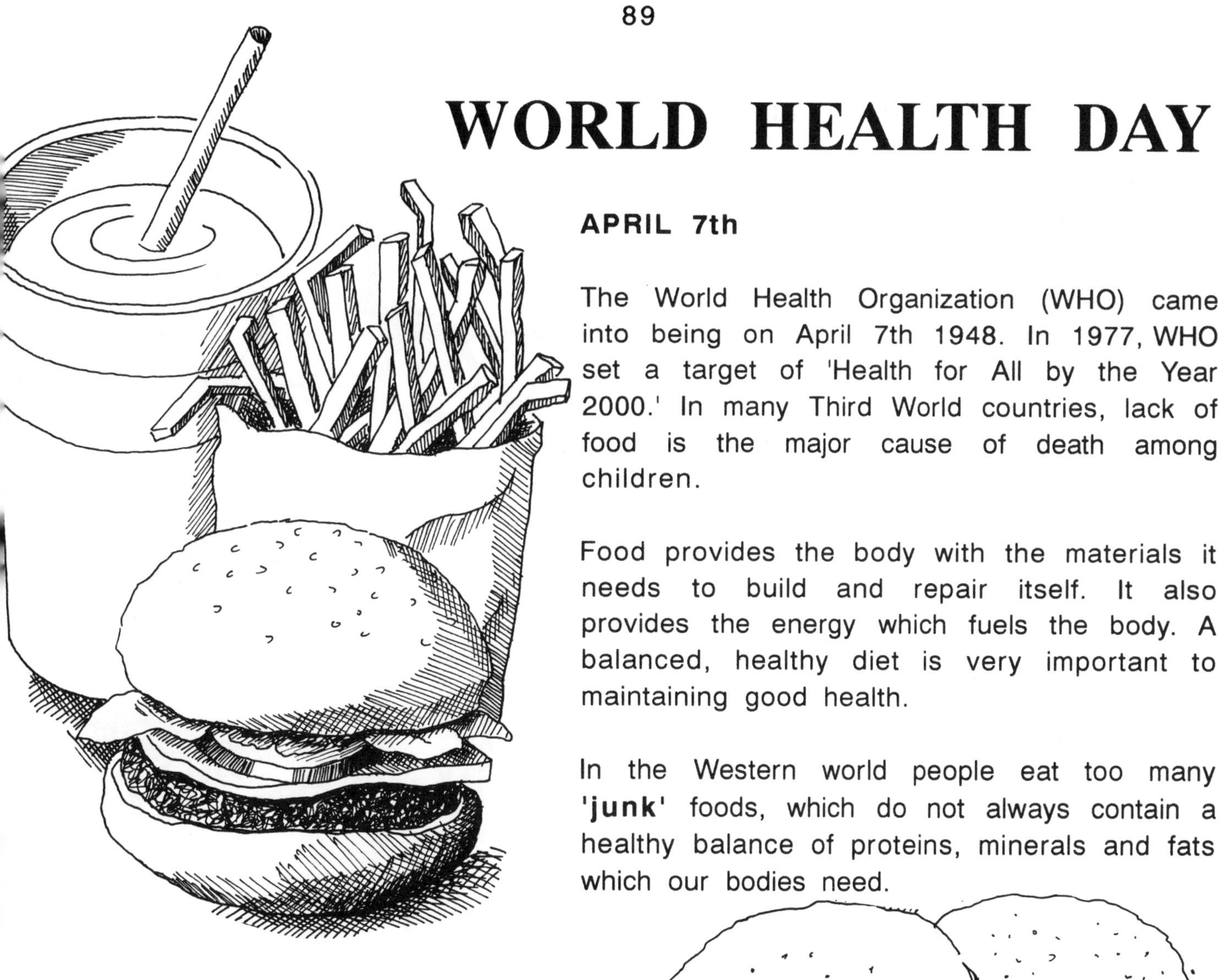

APRIL 7th

The World Health Organization (WHO) came into being on April 7th 1948. In 1977, WHO set a target of 'Health for All by the Year 2000.' In many Third World countries, lack of food is the major cause of death among children.

Food provides the body with the materials it needs to build and repair itself. It also provides the energy which fuels the body. A balanced, healthy diet is very important to maintaining good health.

In the Western world people eat too many **'junk'** foods, which do not always contain a healthy balance of proteins, minerals and fats which our bodies need.

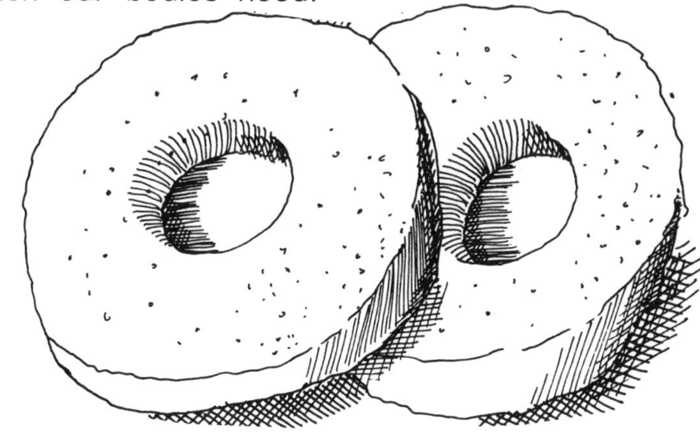

THINGS TO DO

Ask the children to think about which foods they think are good for them and which foods aren't good for them

'WHICH FOODS ARE GOOD FOR ME?' COLLAGE

Collect wrappers from healthy and unhealthy foods and drinks. With the wrappers and cans make a collage. Entitle one side **Healthy Foods** and the other side **Unhealthy Foods**.

'WHATS IN MY FOOD?' COLLAGE

Make a collage of foods showing the different nutrients. Here is a list of some of them:

Carbohydrates produce energy, and are found in, pasta, potato, beans, lentils, nuts, vegetables, fruit, and grains.

Fats are found in dairy products, cooking oils, and meat. Fats not used by the body are stored as body fat.

Proteins, found in pulses, cereals , cheese, bread, milk, fish, nuts, seeds, vegetables (peas, beans and lentils), and meats, help the body to grow and repair.

Fibre, found in cereals, brown bread, brown rice, baked beans, nuts, vegetables, and fruit, help to keep the digestive system in good order.

Minerals such as iron (in bran, wheatgerm, parsley), magnesium (in Brazil nuts, peanuts, almonds), and calcuim (in cheddar, spinach, watercress), help with growth and repair, and are very important for strong bones and teeth.

Vitamins fall into two types: the fat soluble vitamins which are found in fats and oils, meat, fish and dairy products; and the water soluble vitamins which are found in dairy products, cereals, fruit, and vegetables. These with minerals help to regulate the body processes.

Suggested songs: Healthy Learning Songs, published by the BBC Books, BBC Enterprises Ltd., Woodlands, 80 Wood Lane, London W12 OTT. This books comes with a cassette.

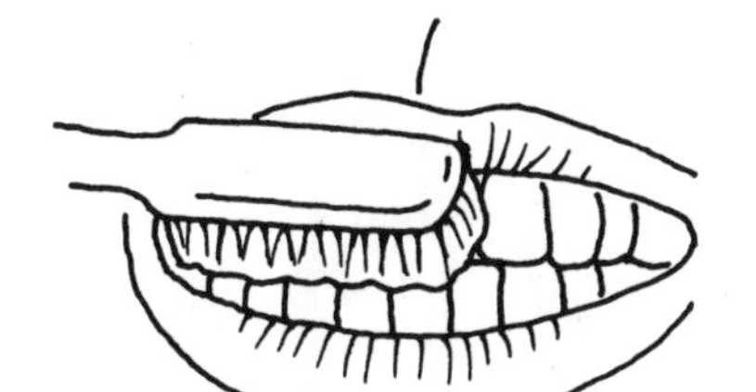

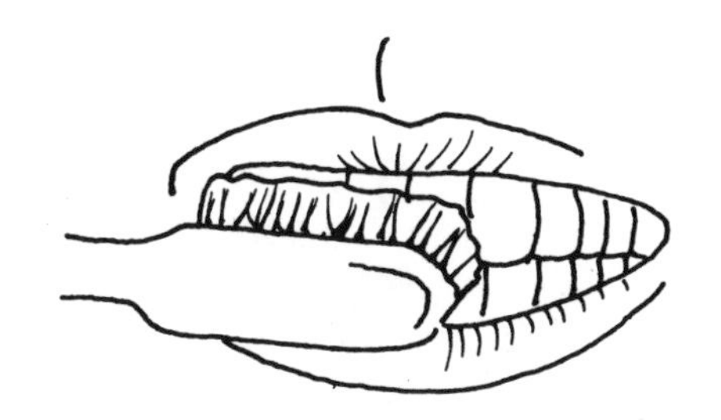

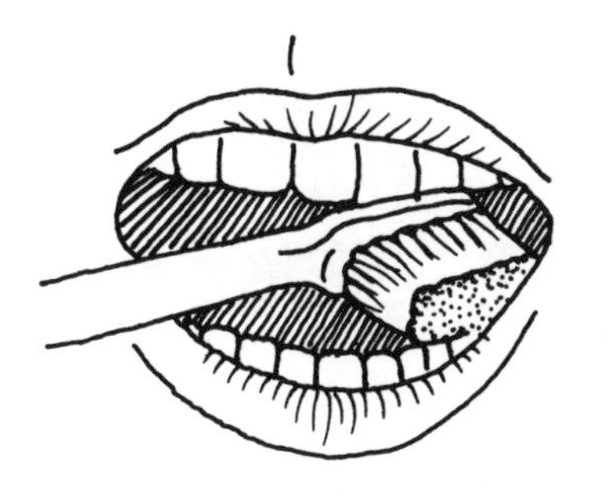

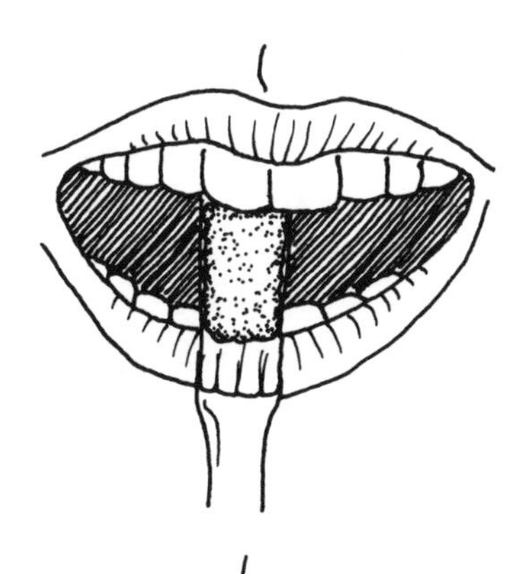

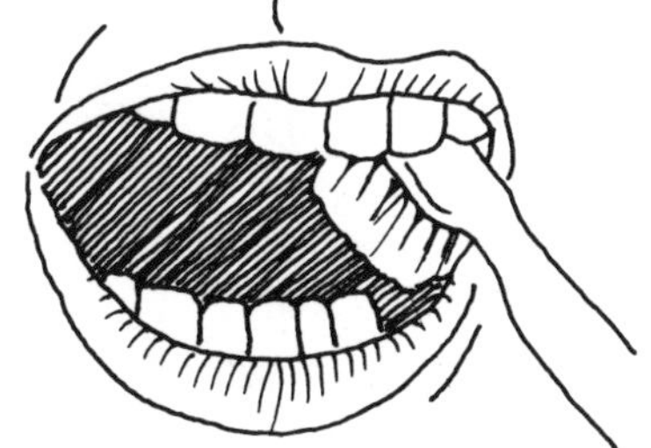

DENTAL CARE

With care nobody need ever have a filling or have their teeth taken out. The cause of both is tooth decay caused by plaque which is a sticky film made up of food and saliva deposits and harmful bacteria. This adheres to the surface enamel area of the teeth.

Sugar is particularly active in helping to form plaque and this is why it is important to talk to them about the importance of brushing their teeth after eating, especially after anything sweet.

THINGS TO DO

Ask a dentist for leaflets on the care of teeth, and make a collage with them. Draw pictures showing the best way to brush your teeth.

Something all children can find fun is to use disclosing tablets. These are harmless tablets that stain the teeth where plaque is present. This will help the children to understand that plaque is invisible.

A GUIDE TO HEALTHY TEETH

1. **Correct brushing.** Brush the top teeth downwards from the gums to the tip. Then brush the bottom teeth upwards. Brush backs of all teeth and gums. Finally, brush biting surfaces backwards and forwards. Brush for at least three minutes but not too hard.

2. **Use fluoride.** This fortifies teeth against plaque, and is found in toothpaste or taken in tablet form.

3. **Regular visits to the dentist.** At least twice a year, even though there might not be anything wrong.

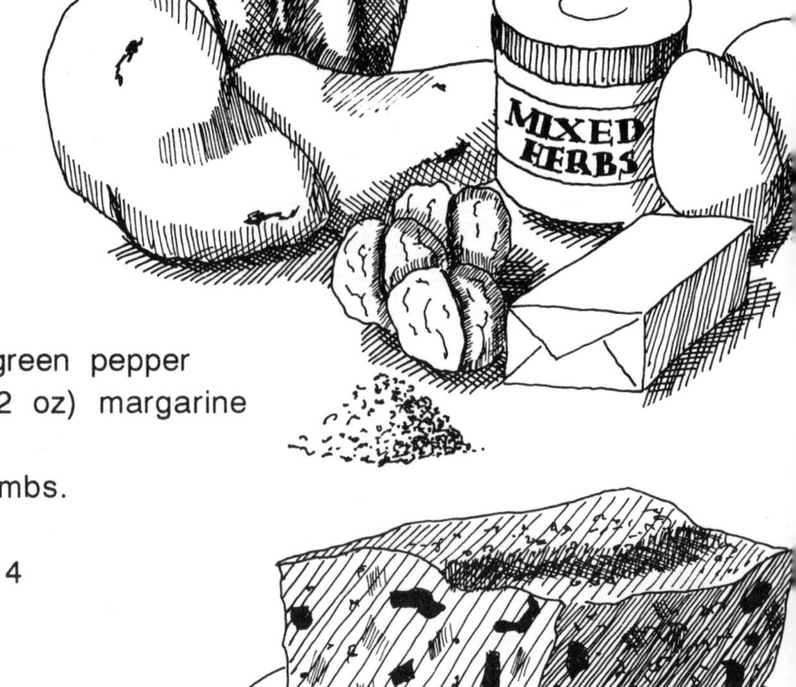

COOKING

POTATO AND WALNUT LOAF

YOU WILL NEED

4 large potatoes
110 g (4 oz) walnuts
2 teaspoons mixed herbs
1 large green pepper
15 g (1/2 oz) margarine
2 eggs
2 tablespoons of wholemeal breadcrumbs.

Oven temperature: 180 'C/350 'F/Gas 4

METHOD

Peel, cook and mash the potatoes. Slice the green pepper and beat the egg. Combine all these with the nuts, herbs and seasoning. Put in a greased loaf tin and top with breadcrumbs and dots of margarine. Bake for 30 minutes.

MUESLI MUNCHIES

YOU WILL NEED

110 g (4 oz) self-raising wholemeal flour
110 g (4 oz) oats
110 g (4 oz) margarine
175 g (6 oz) raw cane sugar
50 g (2 oz) raisins
50 g (2 oz) chopped nuts, raw or roasted
1 large egg, a little milk

Oven temperature: 180 'C/350 'F/Gas 4

METHOD

Cream the margarine and sugar, add the egg. Mix in the flour slowly. Add the rest of the ingredients with milk to make a batter. Drop tablespoons of the mixture on to a greased tray, leaving room for the biscuits to spread, and cook for 10-15 minutes.

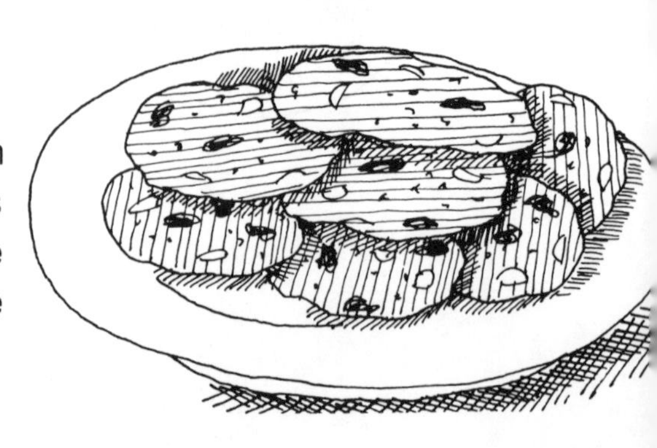

BAISAKHI

APRIL 13th

Baisakhi, meaning April, is the beginning of the new year in India. The celebration is especially important to the Sikhs. In 1699 Guru Gobind Singh wanted to make the Sikhs, faith so strong that they would never denounce it. The guru held a meeting and called for someone who was prepared to give his life for the faith. Daya Ram, who was amongst the crowd, volunteered. The guru took him into a tent and appeared a few minutes later with a blood-stained sword, and then he called for four more volunteers. From the frightened crowd four more men came forward and were taken inside the tent. It was believed that the five men had been killed, but later they reappeared alive, dressed in shining yellow clothes and decorated with weapons.

The guru called these men **Panji Pyare** (five beloved Sikhs), and gave them the surname **Singh** (lion). He called the group **Khalsa** (the pure ones) and baptized them with **amrit** which is made from sugar and water. He then ordered them to maintain five symbols of the faith. These were:

Kesh - uncut hair
Kangha - a comb to fix the hair
Kara - steel bracelet worn on the right wrist
Kara - a short sword
Kaccha - the shorts

The turban and these five articles form a uniform which all Sikhs wear.

Baisakhi is a time when Sikhs who wish to join the fellowship of the Khalsa are baptized at a ceremony called **Amri Chakna**.

Baisakhi lasts for three days, two of which are spent in prayer, singing hymns and giving speeches. On the third day the congregation gathers for the sharing of fruit and **Karah Prasad** (ghee, flour, milk and sugar). And the festival ends with two dances, the **bhangra** danced by the men, and the **giddha** danced by the women. After the ceremony they all eat a vegetarian meal.

THINGS TO DO

A BRACELET

From baker's clay

YOU WILL NEED

4 cups of flour
1 cup of salt
1/2 cup of water
a thin knitting needle
thin elastic

Oven temperature: 180 'C/350 'F/Gas 4

METHOD

1. Mix flour, salt and water together. Knead until firm.

2. Mould the bakers clay into round bead shapes. Make a hole right through each bead with the knitting needle.

3. Carefully place the beads on a baking tray. Bake in the oven for about 1 hour, until lightly brown and firm to the touch.

4. Once the clay has cooled, the children can paint it. For a harder finish coat with varnish. Then thread the beads with elastic and tie to form a bracelet.

MAY

'May brings flocks of pretty lambs,
Sporting round their fleecy dams.'

The Greek goddess Maia gave her name to the month of May. Maia was thought to encourage growth. In her honour, sacrifices were made on the first day of May, accompanied by dancing and merrymaking. Maia has a famous father, Atlas, who is thought to carry the world on his shoulders.

The Anglo Saxons called this month thri-milci (three milk), because the grass became more plentiful, and so the cows were able to give milk three times a day.

MAY DAY

At the beginning of May the Romans used to honour Flora, their goddess of vegetation and flowers. They decorated a tree or maypole, then danced and feasted round it. They brought these customs to Britain, and the maypole became an essential part of the springtime activities.

In medieval times, May 1st was celebrated in England by crowning a May Queen and dancing round a maypole. The Lord of the May, now rarely seen, was once as important as the May Queen. Silk handkerchiefs were tied round his legs and arms. He carried a sword and was completely covered with greenery. He was called Jack-in-the-Green or Jack-in-the-Bush. He was adopted by chimney sweeps, whose annual holiday was on May Day. His name lives on in the sign boards of many pubs called The Green Man.

Preparations for May Day were made the night before, when young people would go out into the countryside and return with armful of flowers and greenery with which to decorate the maypole and the cottages in the village. Maypoles were frequently made of hawthorn, a tree which symbolized joy at the return of summer.

A May Queen and attendants are often chosen to reign over the day's merrymaking. They originally representing Flora and her Nymphs.

In later centuries the Christian Church made links between May and Mary, and then celebrations became religious in tone. Roman Catholics still honour Mary with the title **Queen of May** and have dedicated the month to her.

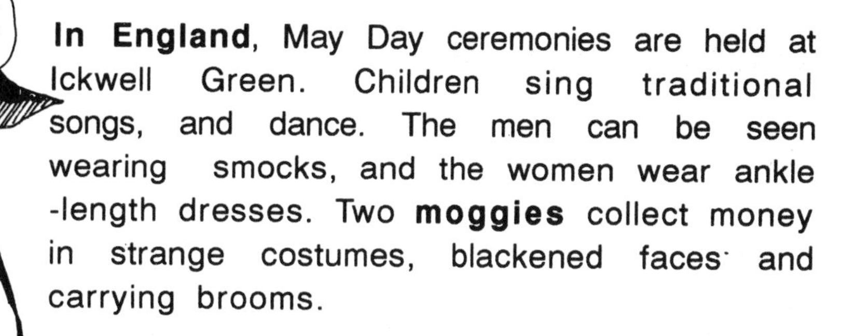

In England, May Day ceremonies are held at Ickwell Green. Children sing traditional songs, and dance. The men can be seen wearing smocks, and the women wear ankle -length dresses. Two **moggies** collect money in strange costumes, blackened faces and carrying brooms.

The maypole on Ickwell's village green is a permanent structure, and dancing around it is one of the highlights of the festival. A May Queen is selected from one of the three villages which take part in the celebration: Ickwell, Caldecote and Warden.

In Russia along the avenues reaching out from Red Square the buildings are decorated with colourful mosaics of gigantic statues of labourers. Since the workers are considered the most important people of the Soviet Union, a special holiday, May Day, honours them. In Moscow there are parades which usually begin as small neighbourhood groups, finally converging in Red Square in a colourful mass of flags and flowers. In Leningrad the focal point of May Day is the Winter Palace of the Czars.

A MAYPOLE SONG

Here's a branch of snowy may,
A branch the fairies gave me.
Who would like to dance today
With the branch the fairies gave me?

Dance away, dance away,
Dance away, dance away
Holding high the branch of may.
Holding high the branch of may.

A traditional song

Suggested songs, **May Garlands, C'est Demain Le Premier Mai**, from **A Musical Calendar of Festivals**, published by Ward Lock Educational.

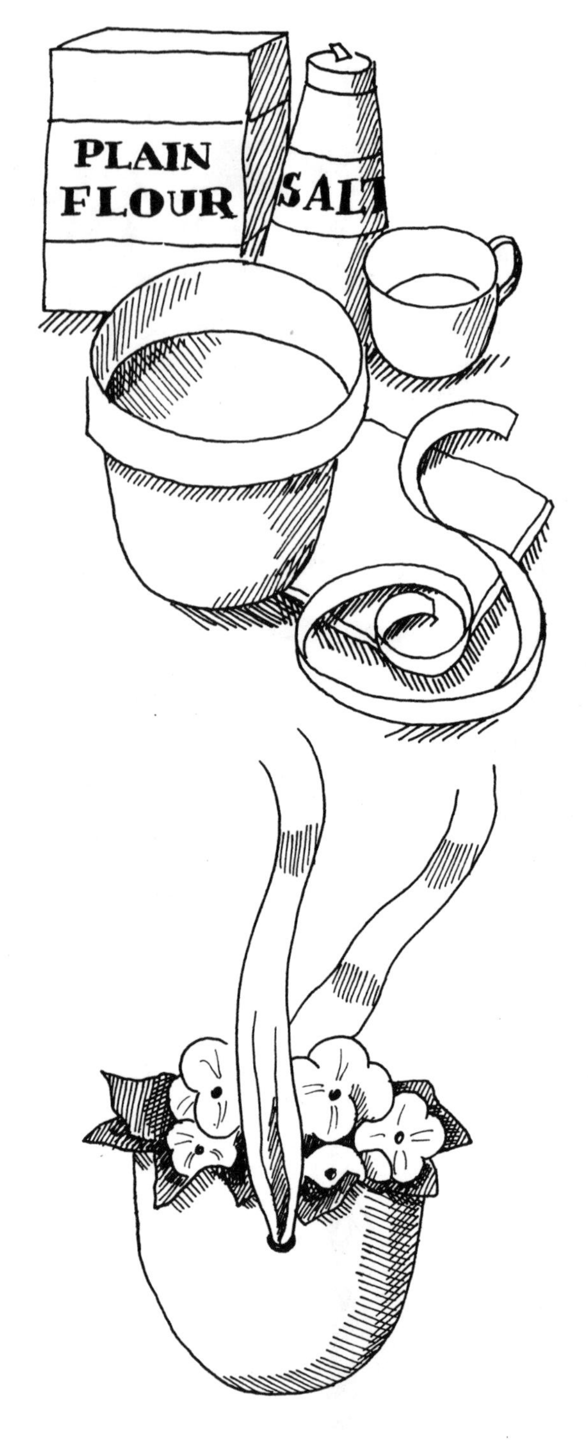

THINGS TO DO

MAY DAY BASKET

In New England, in the United States, May Day baskets are filled with sweets and fresh flowers. They are left on the doorstep of a friend, or hung on the doorknob. The bell is then rung, and the child runs away or hides before he or she is caught.

YOU WILL NEED

4 cups plain flour, 1 cup salt, 1 1/2 cups water, a pudding bowl, tissue paper, ribbon

Oven temperature: 200 'C/400 'F/Gas 6

METHOD

1. Mix the flour, salt and water, kneading it until firm. Roll the dough into a large circle.

2. Grease the outside of the pudding bowl. Carefully place dough around the bowl. Make a hole either side ready for the ribbon. Bake for an hour until lightly brown and firm.

3. Remove the pastry from the bowl and cool. Place the tissue paper all around it. Tie the ribbon through the holes.

COOKING

MAYPOLE CAKE

YOU WILL NEED

175 g (6 oz) flour
175 g 6 oz) margarine
175 g (6 oz) caster sugar
3 beaten eggs
pinch of bicarbonate of soda
1 teaspoon baking powder

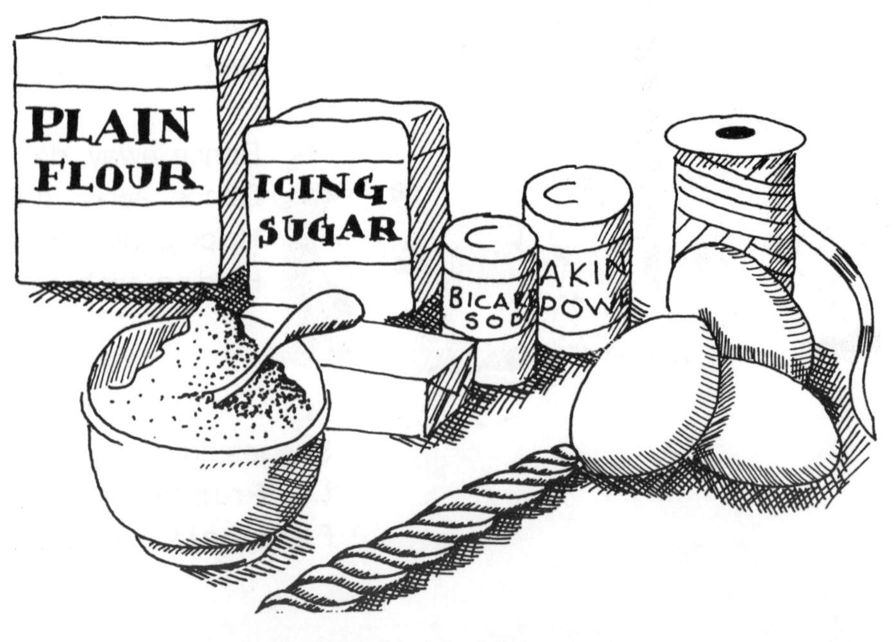

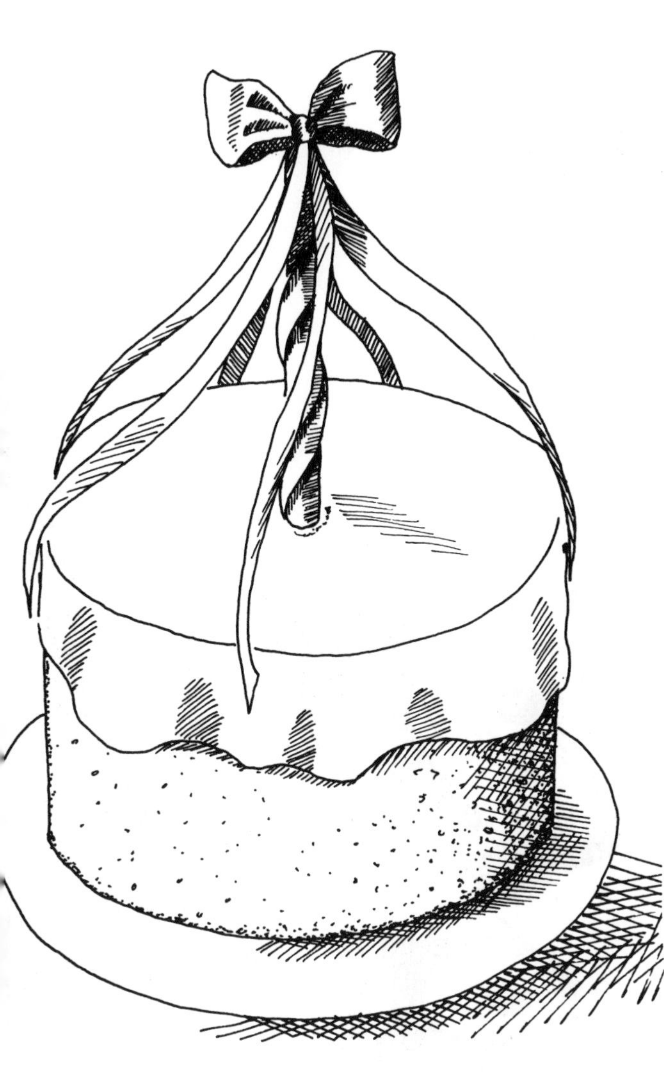

2 tablespoons warm water
icing sugar, ribbons, barley sugar stick

Oven temperature 220 'C/425 'F/Gas 7

METHOD

1. Cream together margarine and sugar. Add flour, bicarbonate of soda, and baking powder. Slowly beat in the eggs and water. Pour into a greased baking tin and cook for 20 minutes.

2. Cool on a rack then ice the cake. For the pole use a stick of barley sugar placed in the middle. From this attach the ribbons.

MAIDS OF HONOUR

YOU WILL NEED

225 g (8 oz) short crust pastry
100 g (4 oz) caster sugar
2 tablespoons raspberry jam
50 g (2 oz) soft butter
100-150 g (4-5 oz) ground rice
1 beaten egg, a few drops almond essence

Oven temperature: 200 'C/400 'F/ Gas 6

METHOD

1. Roll out the pastry and cut into circles. Smear a little raspberry jam on each. Partly cook the tarts in a hot oven for 10 minutes. Remove and allow to cool. Reduce the oven to 180 'C/ 350 'F/Gas 4.

2. Mix the butter, sugar, egg, almond essence, and add enough ground rice to make a stiff paste. Put a spoonful of mixture in each tart case and return to the oven for 25-30 minutes until well risen.

JAPANESE BOYS' DAY

May 5th

Kodomo-no-hi or **Tango-no-sekku**, is a festival for children and a national holiday. Originally it was a festival for boys only. Families with boys put up **koinobori**, or carp streamers, in their gardens and display their samurai warrior dolls called **gogatsun-ingyo** in a room. A banner for each boy in the family is made in the shape of a carp fish and it's painted with bright colours.

The oldest son normally has the largest. The symbol of the carp is chosen because this fish is so strong and brave that it can leap a waterfall and it swims vigorously against the current. Parents hope to see the same qualities in their children. The sword-shaped iris leaf, being symbolic of the spirit of brave warriors, is placed in the boy's bath water.

MY KOINOBORI

My koinobori flies so high,
With its strength to reach the sky.
Black and red, blue and green,
All these colours can be seen.

My carp is strong and oh so brave,
Swims with skill against a wave.
It leaps and dances in the water,
And its courage will never falter.

By Shirley West

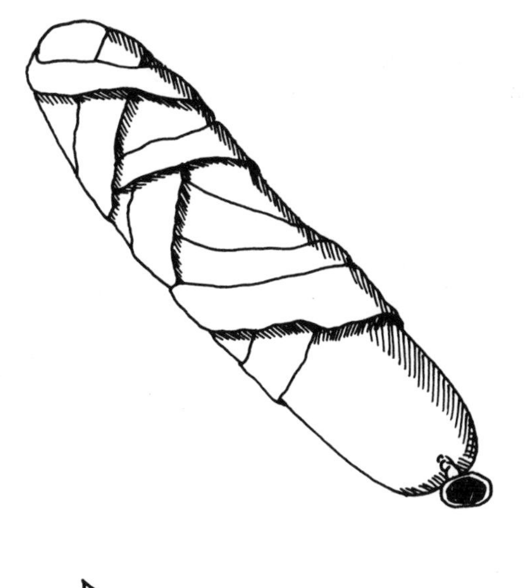

THINGS TO DO

THE KOINOBORI

These are banners in the shape of a colourful carp and made of cloth and paper.

The top is called **fukinagashi,** which is the pennant. The next is called **magoi,** a black carp, representing the father of the house. Then comes **higoi,** a red carp, for the mother. Smaller carps are attached, one for each son.

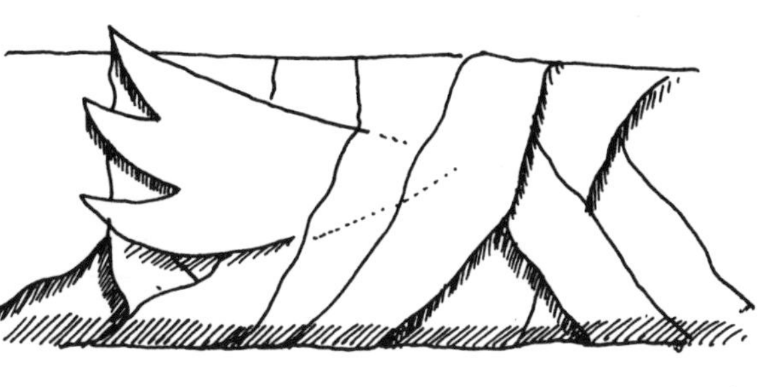

A CARP FISH FOR THE KOINOBORI

<u>YOU WILL NEED</u>

long balloon, newspaper, paste, card, paint, different coloured paper, a long pole

<u>METHOD</u>

1. Tear the newspaper paper into strips and paste several layers on to the balloon to form the carp's body. Cut the card into fin shapes and mould to the fish's body using glued newspaper. Allow to dry for 24 hours

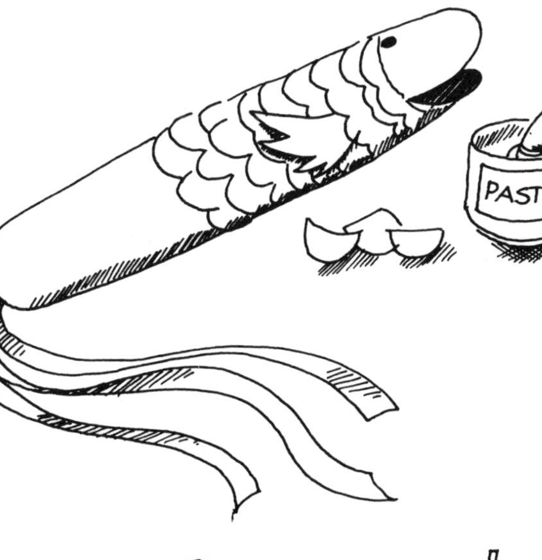

2. Cut out the front of the balloon to form the carps mouth. Make a small hole for the pole above and below the jaw, then paint. Allow to dry.

3. Cut the coloured paper into oval shapes and long streamers. Glue the oval shapes all over the carp's body. Then glue the streamers at the end, and along the carp's back.

4. When it is dry attach the fish to the pole

Suggested songs, **Carp Streamers Fly** from **A Musical Calender of Festivals**, published by Ward Lock Educational.

A SAMURAI MASK AND HELMET

<u>YOU WILL NEED</u>

a round balloon, newspaper, black paper, glue, paint

<u>METHOD</u>

1. Tear the paper into strips and paste several layers on to the balloon. Allow to dry for 24 hours.

2. Cut the balloon in half. Use the first half for the mask by cutting out the features on the face, and paint in bright colours.

3. With the second half make a helmet by cutting a **T** shape as shown. Roll these sections back to form an opening.

4. For the hair, cut the black paper as shown. Allow the children to cut along the lines, then glue this to the back, inside the helmet.

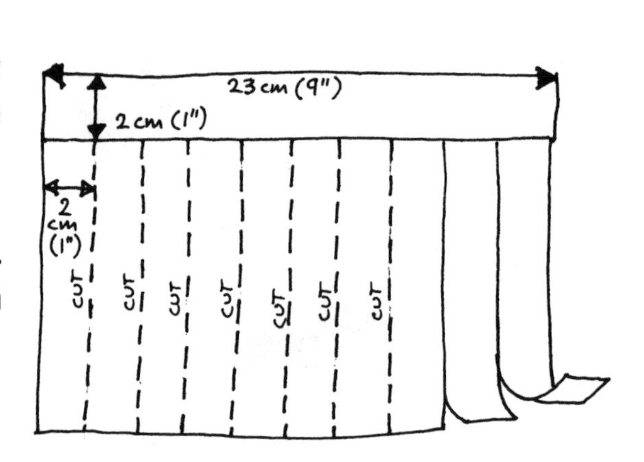

KABUTO HAT from origami

<u>YOU WILL NEED</u>

large square paper, coloured shapes or paint

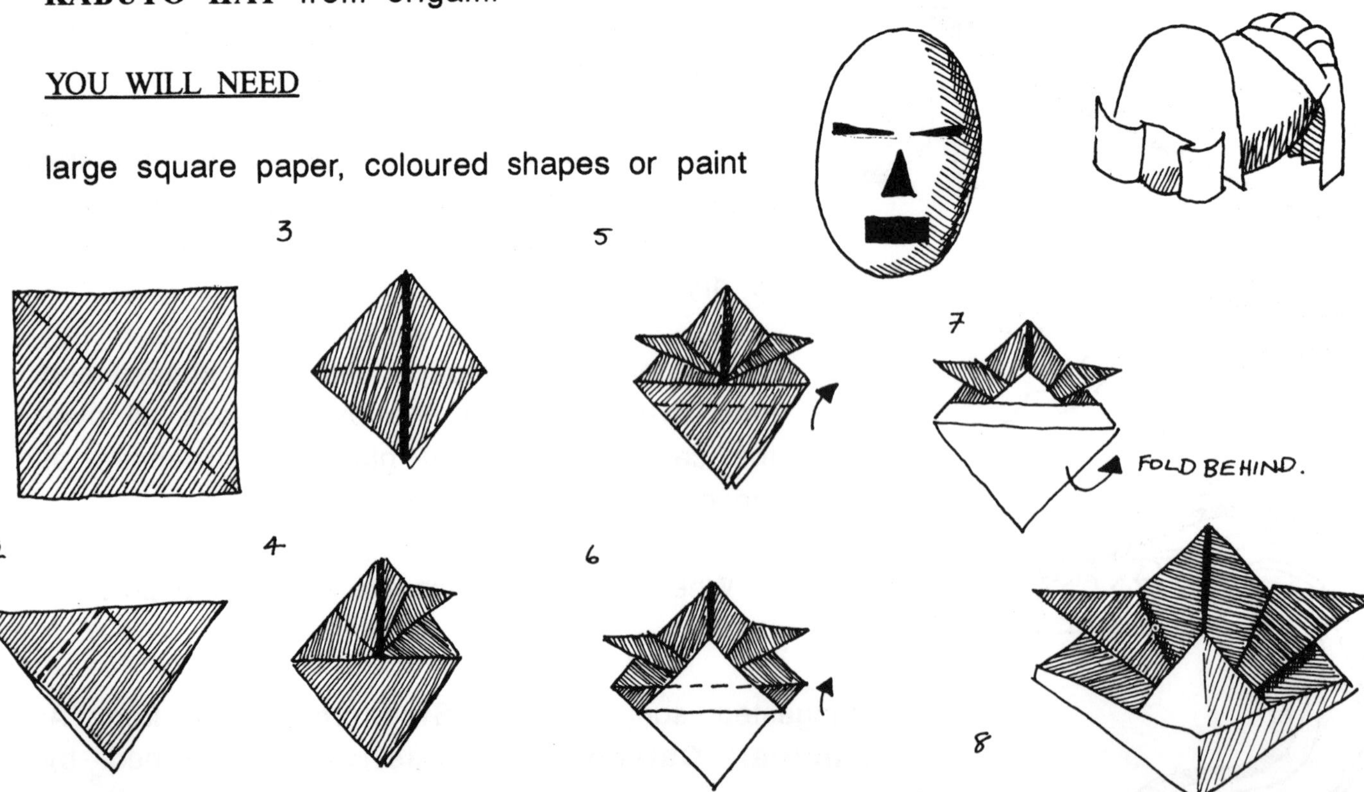

COOKING

Mochi, which area glutinous rice cakes are produced by pounding glutinous rice in a large wooden pot. The chewy white paste that results is shaped into round cakes, and these are eaten as they are, or lightly toasted.

SWEET MOCHI

YOU WILL NEED

250 g (9 oz) rice
470 ml (1pt) water
55 ml (2 fl oz) dark soya sauce
1 tablespoon sugar or honey
25 g (1 oz) sesame seeds
salt

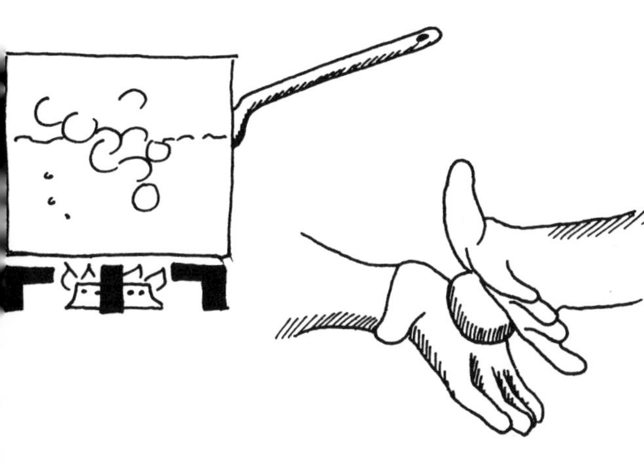

METHOD

1. Wash the rice well and soak in the cooking water for 1 hour. Boil the rice with a little salt until it's very soft.

2. Allow to cool before kneading and pounding the rice. Shape into small balls and this will be a close approximation of rice cakes.

3. Dissolve the sugar or honey and soya sauce in a saucepan over a low heat. Pour into a small bowl.

4. Toast the sesame seeds, crush with a rolling pin and spread in a saucer.

5. Grill the rice cakes for 2-3 minutes either side so that they soften and swell.

6. Dip the rice cakes in the soya sauce and honey mixture, then into the sesame seeds.

DATES OF FESTIVALS AND ANNIVERSARIES

JANUARY

1st	New Year
1st-3rd	Oshogatsu, New Year in Japan
6th	Twelfth Night
17th	The feast of St Anthony
21st Jan - 20th Feb	Chinese New Year
4th Feb - 6th March	Teng Chieh, the festival of lanterns
25th	Burns night in Scotland
Late Jan - early Feb	Saraswati Puja, Hindu festival in India

FEBRUARY

1st	St Bride's Day
2nd	Tu B'Shvat, tree planting in Israel
2nd	Candlemas Day
3rd	Setsuban, the start of spring in Japan
Early Feb	Tet, New Year in Vietnam
7th Feb - 9th March	Mardi Gras/Carnival
14th	Valentine's Day
Late Feb - early March	Purim, a Jewish festival
Late Feb - early March	Shrove Tuesday/ Pancake Day

MARCH

1st	St David's Day in Wales
3rd	Hina-Matsuri, dolls festival in Japan
17th	St Patrick's Day in Ireland
21st	No-Ruz, New Year in Iran
22nd	Holi, Hindu New Year in India
4th Sunday in lent	Mother's Day in Britain
Last day	Oranges and Lemons Day
Late March to April	Easter
Late March to April	Pesach, the Jewish Passover

APRIL

1st	April Fool's Day
7th	World Health Day
13th	Baisakhi, Sikh festival in India
14th	Hefful Day, Cuckoo Day in England
19th	Primrose Day
23rd	St George's Day in England

MAY

1st	May Day
5th	Kodomo-No-Ho, Children's Day in Japan
2nd Sunday	Mothers Day in U. S. A.
Late May - early June	Wesak, Buddhist festival
Late May - early June	Flower Festival in England
Late May - early June	Whitsun
Late May - early June	Shovout, the Jewish Pentecost

JUNE

5th	World Environmental Day
5th	Dragon Boat Festival (Ch'u Yuen)
14th	Flag Day in America
14th	Father's Day
21st	Midsummer Day

JULY

4th	American Independence Day in U. S. A.
7th	Tanabata, Japanese Star Festival
15th	St Swithin's Day
Late July-August	Raksha Bandhan, a Hindu festival
July-September	Janmashtami, Hindu festival

AUGUST

1st-2nd week	Ghana's Yam Festival
Early August	Raksha Bandhan

SEPTEMBER

1st-9th	Chinese Kite festival
Early September	Ganesh's birthday, a Hindu festival
Mid-late	Rosh Hashanah, a Jewish festival
Mid-late	Yom Kippur, a Jewish festival

OCTOBER

Around 15th	Harvest Festival
24th	United Nations Day
Late Oct-early Nov	Diwali, Hindu Festival of Light
31st	Hallowe'en

NOVEMBER

2nd	All Souls' Day
5th	Guy Fawkes Day
15th	Shichigosan, Japanese Feast Day
Mid November	Guru Nanak's, a Sikh festival
Last Thursday	Thanksgiving in America
30th	St Andrew's Day in Scotland

DECEMBER

6th	Festival of St Nicholas
13th	St Lucia's Day in Sweden
Mid December	Hanukkah, Jewish Festival of Light
25th	Christmas Day
26th	Boxing Day
26th	St Stephen's Day in Ireland
31st	Hogmanay in Scotland

THE MUSLIM YEAR

This is approximately ten days shorter than the Western year. The Islamic Calendar is lunar, which means that each new month begins with the appearance of the new moon at Mecca. Therefore Ramadan varies annually, and may occur in winter or summer. This way fasting does not always take place during the same season, so that Muslims around the world have a fair turn of hardship during long, hot days and then colder, shorter days. Officially, Islam recognizes only two festivals, those being Id Al-Fitr which marks the end of the fast of Ramadan, and Id Al-Adha the festival of sacrifice.

Ramadan starts at the appearance of the crescent moon and lasts between twenty nine and thirty days. Here is a guide to the starting date of Ramadan during the 1990s.

1991	February 20th
1992	February 10th
1993	January 31st
1994	January 21st
1995	January 11th
1996	January 1st
1997	December 22nd
1998	December 12th
1999	December 2nd
2000	November 22nd